YOUR GUIDE TO SELF-IMPROVEMENT

Become An Entrepreneur Of Your Life

GEORGE M. WALLACE

CONTENTS

INTRODUCTION
Self-improvement Is A Journey

Self-improvement is indeed a journey with many winding roads; some may lead you to new adventures while others take you to danger. Therefore you always need a road map that will set you on the right course and take you where you need to go. The premise of this book is to improve with practical steps and tools to get you there. Have you ever seen people who have everything put together? They have the house on the hills and a car that makes people feel far behind in life. Yet they also seem to be happy all at the same time while others are still trying to get their foot in the door.

I've seen it a million times, having worked with entrepreneurs, CEO's and business people that the first step to achieving your desired result is to know what you want from life and to set a plan, a course of action to take. Let's put it this way; you cannot get going towards your goal if you hope to get there; it has to be on purpose.

By that I mean it has to be intentional. How does one then get to their pinnacle of success? The answer to this question indeed lies in the daily routines in your life. It lies in how you manage and organize your life, and it also lies in your need to want to improve.

I want you to take a moment to imagine yourself in 5, 10, or 15 years and tell me what comes forth to the front of your mind? Is it a large house where your beautiful family is happily enjoying a carefree Sunday? Or perhaps you imagined that you were not tied down by responsibilities or a need for a job, you did not have a manager breathing down your neck waiting for the next project. Or maybe you saw yourself traveling the globe, meeting people in every corner of this beautiful earth? The most important aspect of your future is that you are content. You are happy that you reached this point, and once you know that's what you want from life, you can work backward, add the strategies, add the tactics and dig into to do the work to make it a reality. Therefore, I started this book by saying that self-improvement is a journey.

I don't mean that in the way that life's a journey. I mean it in that self-improvement is a path you must walk on within your life personally, spiritually, and professionally to get what you want. Sure, if you're going to work in an office for the next 20 years, collect your retirement and go on that vacation you've meant to take, you can do it the traditional way and get great at life. Or you can take the path that many before have walked. You may even have seen the rewards unfold in front of them. They have sought out a truly separate life and built for success, they aimed for never ceasing discipline and improvement, and they knew that being an entrepreneur of their life was at the heart of every decision they made.

In this book, you will learn many fundamentals about

improving yourself and preparing for success. You will discover that you must take control as you go through life. It would help if you did not let life sway you as it bends the winds of change. The onus is on you to always take charge, make the changes, and be the difference you hope to see at every stage of your life. You may see this as life prompting you to get out of your comfort zone; then, you must do that. Taking control is all about introspection that can tend to be painful. It can be tough and is not for the faint of heart, and that is the sole reason I wanted to start with the concept of "taking control." Naturally, if you do not take control of your life, others will, and you will be left in the backseat of your own life, going slowly nowhere. Once you've shifted the car into the right gear, your foot is off the pedal, and you are entirely in control of your current situation, then it's time to start creating a plan, a goal.

Every successful person in life has an end goal, the one that they look at, and it spurs them to do better. Now when you think of your goal, I want you to ask yourself: "Is my destination inspiring and exciting?" or you could ask, "Does my goal get me out of bed in the morning?". Once you can answer with a resounding "yes" on both questions, I think you can safely say you have a worthy destination. Once you have a goal in mind, a calmness will settle, and you will have no other option but do everything in your power to get to your destination. In this section, I want to show you how you harness that idea of a goal and help it bring self-improvement into your life.

Taking control and having a destination is not enough. That's the first step, but if you want to be the sole owner of your life on your terms, you absolutely must increase your productivity. At this stage, I want to pause and ask you a question that may shed some light on your productivity levels. Answer this: "How many hours do you spend playing video games or watching TV?" If you said it was more than 2 hours a day, you might need some help getting more productive and using the essential tools I'll share in this section. Being a productive person is not always about work output, but it's an important aspect. It's not still about people seeing that you are getting stuff done. No, it's more than that - it's a lifestyle that you foster that you build, and that boosts your income, your station in life, and gives you the confidence and competence to keep going.

The ideas I mentioned above are essential but will not work unless you start to build networks and leverage those networks. How do you do that? Well, you have to start engaging with people. The right people that can move your current business or work projects forward are not just any people. This area is often called having a level of interpersonal skills, and it talks about how well you engage with people. It also helps tremendously for you to build your likeability factor because people prefer being around others who have interpersonal skills versus those who do not. But don't worry if you lack in this area. I have devoted an entire chapter to improving your interpersonal skills, and I'm sure it will maximize your relationships and improve your communication skills tenfold.

Once you've invested in interpersonal skills, you would be all set to keep on improving, and that means devoting yourself to the craft of continuous improvement. It could mean you have to learn a new language, apply for a new degree, or engage your boss for a new promotion. These are endless ways to spring up on your path that could be the stepping stone for you. That said, if you are not continually improving, you will not have access to them. Others will overtake you, and you will be worse off. But it doesn't have to be that way. There are time tested tools that will support you in your endeavor to keep on improving.

Over time you may have kept moving forwards and seen continuous improvement shape your life and make it better but even more that you need to improve your station in life. That's a matter of taking the next step in your work, business, or personal experience. It's saying that you want to progress ahead and commit to building yourself and getting ready for what is ahead. While many people decide to stagnate and keep on living monotonous lives, you can keep building and grow for the better. After the journey of introspection, action, and progress, the final chapter will set its sights on a tall order. By that, you will learn how to push your boundaries and listen to your inner voice. You will learn to persevere and stay the course even when times are seemingly hopeless. This section will give you the know-how and practical guides I have personally used to make this happen. It would help if you were continually on the lookout for complacency and laziness, and the best way to do that is to introduce a habit of pushing your boundaries. If you don't push your limits, then nobody else will, so it's up to you to strive for more and do more at every stage of your life. You are the captain of this ship called your life.

I wanted to give you a taste of what to expect within the pages of this book. So please read this book, knowing that I've walked this path of self-improvement before. It was challenging, and as with most things, it can be even more challenging to stay the course. It's painful but not impossible. You have the tools that you can use and keep growing to improve yourself. It's latent, within you, and waiting for you to draw it out. Your solution lies within you, but you also need a little nudge, which is why reflection and reading can be quite helpful to bring up new insightful connections within your brain. I hope you bought this book, knowing that it will bring advice that has been tried and tested. Also, I hope this book brings you towards your path of self-improvement. Everyone has a unique way of getting there, and this guide will ignite your path. Join me as we take a walk through the chapter that will help you take control. This is the starting point.

CHAPTER 1
Take Control

When you think of taking control, you may be prone to imagine a flustered person who has simply let their entire career and home deteriorate. When I talk about control, it's not that you may be out of control but that there is a level of ultimate equilibrium needed in your life for you to be your best self. This is the best version of you that will help you thrive under most circumstances.

Have you ever been in that situation where you know that you must get everything done, create a plan, and feel like you will reach your goals; however, most of the ideas do not come to fruition? Why is that? You may have missed a couple of deadlines, and your manager is concerned about your work performance. It may be due to procrastination or a lack of motivation for your job at present. It's causing you to delay the great work and progress you have made already.

Therefore, there comes a time when you have to pause and understand what may have gone wrong. In this chapter, I want to help you build awareness about your life situations that may be holding you back from your goals and reaching success.

Contents

Defining control

Control, by definition, means that you have the power to ensure that something either personally or professionally runs smoothly. You made it so. In your home life, it may be that you are always in control of how you design your household and what furniture to bring in. Also, because you pay the rent, it may be that you can easily decide to move to another place. You have full control of your home life. Alternatively, you may live with someone, and you share the household responsibilities, and in this way, there is dual control, so you must convene and make decisions on how your home life moves together.

Let's consider that from a work context. You have a manager at the office, and you will often only be following orders unless you are the boss. You don't have much control over the work that you do as it's predefined, nor do you do your salary or your manager. At times you may have control of your dress code if that is allowed. But you see a company makes the regulations and rules and employee's stick to it. Therefore I want to show you in this section that being in control is

10

relative to your situation.

You may then ask:" Where am I in full control" As I mentioned above, it would be in your home life and what you own for your life. Another area would be within yourself. The decisions you make that concern your well being and future always reside within you and your framework. You have to think through every problem, then also face those consequences. If something does not work out, well, you are responsible for it, and if it is a success, you get the accolades. So, control in this chapter's context is the control that you possess, and that is innate to you.

A person can either be in control or out of control in their life. If you're out of control, it may well be that something has happened to you recently. Perhaps you did not get the promotion you worked so hard for, or you're going through a divorce or do not feel stimulated. Many reasons could make you feel out of control. Yet it generally looks like it's a messy state of affairs, where an out of control person may do irrational things, and create situations that impact people negatively. Understandably it is a challenging process to get back to a state of normalcy when things are simply not going your way. But if you stay in a state of no control of your life, things only get worse. As they say, the best way out is through.

Let's now compare being out of control with being in control. What does that look like? This is a more tame sort of situation where someone who is in control always looks put together in their personal and professional life. They look like they invested time and energy into their appearance, and they also look like a problem solver. This is key because they have control, then people tend to rely on them to help them and get the job done. Think about the last project in your business or at work. Who did your manager choose to head it up? If you said that it was the most organized and trustworthy person, you would see a trend. People, and especially executives and business owners want to work with people who are organized and well put together as they need someone reliable.

That's a comparison to get us to think about control from opposite ends of the spectrum. Then you may be prone to ask the all too important question:" How do I take control?"

The truth is that as humans, we always crave the feeling of control. If you think back to our ancient ancestors that created enclosures of communities to feel safe and build our foundations of civilization, their need was always to be in control, whether against the harsh elements or the predators. Even more so, you will see it within the structures of society. We are predisposed to organize and make sure there is control within our communities. So too, you possess the genetic makeup of our ancestors who had an innate need to take control of life.

Taking control is innate to you, and can be done once you have self-awareness. The self-awareness is simply that feeling to look at your actions and understand they may not always be serving you well. It's how you perceive yourself and what you've done and the courage to recognize that you can improve. In his bestselling book Emotional Intelligence,

Daniel Goleman emphasizes that you have an innate ability to understand your feelings and moods so that it helps you get what you hope to achieve. It paints the picture that being out of control in your work life can result from your emotions or the inability to handle them appropriately.

For example, let's say you had a bad day at work, and you're worried your performance is not up to scratch. You can handle it in one of two ways. Either you can resiliently push forward and work that much smarter or get down in the dumps and complain to anyone who will listen. Now, if you take the complaining route, you may inadvertently be impacting your ability to take control. You are saying that others are affecting your livelihood instead of taking responsibility for your work. Yet, if you are prone to deflect the blame, you can always choose not to. You can want to take control instead of being controlled by a situation.

How to take control

Over the years, it's become more and more apparent that the world is getting more complex and stressful. Our old coping mechanisms, such as working more to meet the demands, simply do not work as well as they used. Therefore you need to employ better systems to help you take control of your life to make you feel more confident and joyful in your work. When you take control of your situation, it will look like you enjoy your work in a more meaningful manner than you had done before.

Build Confidence -In the first part, to take control, you must be confident. This is the pillar of being in control. A person who is not sure will not have the ability to improve and get better at work. A person who is not confident will be too afraid to make mistakes, and a person who is not sure will falter at the first signs of criticism. Yet confidence can be an up and down cycle. You know some days you feel up and ready to take on the world while others can simply be an uphill battle that destroys all motivation. The good news is that there is an excellent formula for building your confidence and maintaining that confidence.

Get things done - The more you leave something to the last minute, the more they will pile up and you will feel less productive and proactive. The brain starts to sense a threat when deadlines are close immediately, and you fail to finish the project. You even begin to see a sense of lethargy that collects within you, making it harder to start. It's always the momentum of achieving. The more you achieve and tick off, the more confident you will be. Think about how you feel when you submit a project on time and of a high standard. It probably feels great knowing you could get the work done, and that feeling taps into your sense of intrinsic motivation to keep on doing and getting better along the way. You start to see yourself as a person who is consistently doing more and getting the job done. And guess what? Others will begin to see you in the same way.

Track how you're doing - It may seem like a chore at first to track your progress and how you are getting along, but it could be a devil disguised as a tedious task. You have to understand that when you monitor yourself, it's you telling yourself that you've progressed, it's you making plans, and it's you committing to keep going. Remember that it is the best way to reach those massive goals because you break them down and make the tasks easier. They become mini-goals that serve to fuel your momentum towards the bigger goals. As an example, you may be creating a work project that will last two months, but looking at the massive pile of work is demotivating and can kill your spirit. Instead, you may decide to break down the tasks into segments and attach deadlines to those. That's much more manageable and more enticing. The bonus is that you get to experience wins along the way.

Be a good person - There is always the easy way and the hard way, but if you never do the right thing, it will impact you down the line. A person who does the right thing may take longer to reach their goals than someone who decided to take shortcuts. While they may not see it now but if you look 5, 10, or 15 years down the line, you will see that the impact is vast. Being a good person is about having integrity, always keeping your promises, and yes, doing the right thing even when nobody's looking. You may decide not to cut corners on a project or limit spending on the company card for personal items.

Fear exists - Remember that fear will always be there, but you don't have to allow it to rule your life. It's there to help us detect danger and to keep you moving forward, but it is also a primal emotion that can hinder you if you let it. Things that create fear would be dreading a job loss when there is no clear evidence or worrying about your business unnecessarily instead of taking some sort of action that will help steady your business and keep it moving. And while you cannot be fearless, you can know that fear is there and that you have to do the work despite the fear. You always have the choice, and you can choose to embrace the fear and let it become your friend.

Don't be a push-over - I understand it can be scary to have your say and have people judge you. You may fear you lose your job by being the person who goes against the grain. The truth is that the more you let people dictate to you and give you more work, then your dreams also take a backseat. You invest more time worrying about what other people think versus worrying about your expectations and vision for your life. Start small by saying no to things that are not part of your job, slowly migrate to more prominent activities like talking to a spouse who may also be hindering your progress.

Remove procrastination

We're all guilty of this aspect of life, knowing that there are so many things to do but choose to do something easy. The habit may have started in college, where you know you had an assignment due but opted to hang out with your friends instead. These days, it could be that you know you should spend time crafting business proposals or working on your business but decide to watch YouTube or play games. These may be exciting things at the time, but they do you a disservice. They do that by taking you away from the actions that could help you achieve your dreams. These activities hinder progress, and procrastination can become a habit if you do not put a plan in place to curb it.

This will help you get rid of procrastination in your life:

Know that you are procrastinating - Once you can get a sense that you may be delaying, it becomes easier to curb it. You can observe yourself and monitor daily what you do. Think of writing your to-do items in a journal daily and watch how much progress you make every day. Look back, see how many to-do items have been missed, and think about low priority tasks supporting your procrastination.

Understand why you are procrastinating - Some procrastinate because they don't enjoy the work they do and so it takes them longer to complete it. Others procrastinate because they have an inherent fear that the output will not be good enough. You must figure out if you fit into any of these categories, to begin with, as it can then help you unpack the derailers of you taking control of your life. Once you can confirm, you can then start to create strategies that will prevent you from procrastinating in the future.

Start doing - I know it can be easier said than done, but I've found that once you put effort into eliminating procrastination, then you feel committed to the goal at large. You give it your all and start supporting yourself instead of shooting yourself in the foot. As a starting point, you should aim to forgive yourself for procrastinating in the past. This will help set your mind free to focus on tangible actions, like creating systems that prevent procrastination. First, you must keep a to-do list with five activities every day and make sure you do them by the end of that day. You can use an electronic device or choose to use a pen and paper. Once you complete a task, scratch it off the list. Next, aim to prioritize your task accordingly so that you always accomplish the most critical first. Many apps can help you schedule and prioritize, as well as work effectively. A good example is Todoist and Focus. The Todoist app helps you keep all your tasks in one place and prioritize them while Focus is an app that allows you to work using the Pomodoro technique.

Get your financial life in order

I found a recent study that shows that households in the US who had high levels of debt were more prone to have stress issues, and that results in a lack of confidence. Yet, this can be remedied by choosing to look at the state of your finances at present. You can then figure out how to improve it. It starts by taking all of your bank accounts, credit cards, and debt and understanding how everything looks on paper. I use the app Mint, which helps me organize everything in my bank account, expenses, and spending to give me an idea of my financial situation. It does this automatically, so I don't have to do it. And I've seen some alarming data over three months. Yet, it was beneficial to understand my financial situation and then to make a plan. As a starting point, you should save for an emergency fund in case something may happen in the future. I recommend $1000 if you are still paying down debt. If you have no liability, you should crank up your emergency fund to 6 months of living expenses. This becomes quite helpful in case you experience a sudden job or a crisis in your personal life.

Get and stay healthy

Becoming healthy is a buzz phrase right now, but the benefits cannot be emphasized enough. Exercising for 30 minutes a day is recommended for being physically and emotionally fit. Additionally, it helps with your stress and can also boost your levels of confidence. The idea of exercising is not a strange one as people have been doing it for centuries. Earlier it used to be about walking leisurely, and now people visit gyms regularly to keep fit. Some are executives, and others are university students aiming to keep the pounds off and the stress at bay. This is a sure-fire way also to give you a boost in your mood.

Learn how to deal with stress

One of the most significant investments you can make in life is finding out your stressors and how to cope with them. You will certainly not eliminate them, but you can find ways to manage them. There are a few options that are available such as practicing mindfulness. Mindfulness is about doing regular activities with more awareness and being in the moment. For example, when you make tea, instead of mindlessly doing it, you should observe the water boiling, the pouring of the water, and how the tea's texture feels. This done a few times a day can relieve stress immensely. Alternatively, you can also use Headspace, which offers daily free meditations to support your stressful lifestyle.

Key takeaways

Taking control of your life and the situations in them are

vital to how you thrive in life. When you understand that you are always in control of what happens to you, it changes how you view situations and helps you handle them better.

There are five key ways to take control: to build confidence, get your financial life in order, understand, and stay healthy, and deal well with stress.

Building your confidence may seem daunting at first, but little actions can make a big difference. The first step is knowing yourself and what makes you feel less than confident. Once you understand this, you can use our practical steps to fix the low confidence factor.

Getting your finances in order may be the best decision of your life, and the goal is to use simple methods at first to remove financial pressure from your life.

Keeping fit is one way to look healthy, but also it will help chase the blues away and help keep you in control of how you look.

Stress comes in many shapes and sizes, but know that everyone experiences it at some point in their life. The essential part of stress is that you have the innate ability to handle it by using mindfulness and meditation.

Actions steps

1. Make a list of your life's areas that are important to you, such as your physical health, finances, and family life. You can add more as well as each person has a setlist of what's essential and what's not.
2. Use that list to rank the priority for you. Then give yourself a score on how you think you have done in these areas. The score of one would be poor, and five would be great.

3. Now that you know how you're doing choose a tool in this section to get started on improving the first item on your list.

CHAPTER 2
Have A Destination

Having a destination in mind can prove to be daunting as you venture forth on your path to success. At time's you think it may prove to be bad luck to fixate on a destination, but I would like to clarify this idea of a destination. The destination means your goal in the grand context of self-improvement. It means your ultimate vision for your life and could even relate to the reason you wake up every day and work at a job or run your own business. This is the core topic of this chapter, where we will discuss your current and final destinations to success.

Contents

The destination defined
Visualization
Persistence

The destination defined

You may be looking out towards your future, wondering if it will be a successful few years or one riddled with many challenges. There seems to be apathy at present for the future, yet I've seen so many changes over the decades where businesses thought they would not make it for another year. That belief system inherently derailed their progress.

That belief system stopped them from attaining the final destination they so desired. For example, consider a company that has stood the test of time, such as Procter and Gamble. You may know them as a company specializing in many commodities like shampoos, diapers, and more. Yet did you know that they have been around since 1837? It all started because of James Gamble and William Procter, who were brothers-in-law and one sold soap, the other candles. They invested some money to build a business called Procter and Gamble, and after about a year, were making millions of dollars. Yet, their idea was rooted in this concept of having a destination, and that was to make the best products that would help people and enhance their lives. They innovated, and they always brought new and useful products to market, intending to stay ahead of the curve. This is one example where staying the course and having a stable destination in mind will get you far.

I also think that having a destination is all about planning your life a few years ahead. Some people plan a year while others have their lives mapped out for 5 to 10 years. Some people want to be financially free while others want to travel the world. Everyone is seeking a destination that brings them happiness. Happiness can be so many things to so many people. It's a very subjective concept, yet many people agree that contentment is also an excellent destination. When people are on their deathbed, they always look back from their current target and wish they had done more. So in finding a destination and a goal for yourself, you can avoid having any such regrets as you get older. There is also a different way to look at this idea.

Some people like to imagine their funeral day and seek to establish what people would say about them. They want to know that people said they were good people, or that they served their community or that they had lots of wealth and their families lived a beautiful life along the way. In this way, the idea is to look forward to where you currently are and finding what is closest to your heart and your desire for success.

So our focus should then be looking at yourself far into the future and observing our best selves. Right now, there are many aspects of your life you don't particularly like. You may be sitting in a mansion, but you never have work-life balance. Therefore you would like to have an experience where your work does not control your life, and you can spend as much time as you wish with your family. On the other end of the spectrum, someone else may be enjoying life, but they are working 18 hour days for low pay. They would kill to live in a mansion and have the luxuries afforded in that lifestyle. It shows that everyone's ultimate destination is different and unique to their situation. The difference is then how you plan for your future, and what are the tools you use to bring a new narrative into your current existence.

If you are currently unhappy, no amount of complaining will fix the problem of unhappiness. But then what can fix your problems to get to a different destination? First, we'll need to define that problem in a meaningful way. Einstein was famous for once stating that "a problem well defined is a problem half solved" and what he meant was that you should take time to work at the challenge you currently face in your life and know that you can update it. You should know that the problems you have now cannot be fixed with the mindset or the same thinking you had a while ago. You need to update your methods of visualization to show what you truly want. So while the problem must be defined, also what you genuinely wish for must be set too. You can see how that becomes challenging, but it's entirely possible to find a point where your current problem can be defined to give you the answer in making your next move.

Let's start by looking at the concept of visualization.

Visualization

I'm sure that when you think about this idea of visualization, it makes you think about unlocking what's within your mind's eye. You know it has to do with a view of something, but right now, you don't quite understand the specifics and also how it can help you define your destination. Visualization is, in fact, a formulation of a mental image of something. In other words, anything in your mind can be a visualization. In that way, you can have useful visualizations and negative visualizations. How is that possible? Well, in your life you will not always have good experiences.

As a child, you may have experienced something negative

that was imprinted in your mind, so you shifted and changed and adapted to these situations. You may think that those memories have been long gone, but they are in everything you do. They make up your psyche and also impact your behavior and your belief systems. Your belief systems are your core values and how you engage with most situations in the world. This lies in the inner workings of your mind.

Yet you can always improve your visualizations, and this does take effort and time but can yield many benefits along the way. The first benefit is that when your mindset is fuelled with positive visualizations, you become someone who infuses these decisive moments into your life. Little by little, you move the negative displays deeper into your mind so that you update your mindset. This update can be thought of as a software update on your computer. At first, you get those messages to upgrade, but you are too busy, so you ignore it until one day, your system slows down. You cannot use the applications or research info on the internet.

Your system update should have been done ages ago, but because you neglected it now, you have more challenges. It may be that you have to meet a work deadline or send an important email urgently, but because you cannot use your computer, it will have to wait. Similarly, your mind is always in need of an update and gives you many warning signs along the way. It could be that you get symptoms of apathy or a loss of joy for your work. But you do not heed it until one day you have burnout because of a lack of vision or purpose. Now you have to start doing the hard work to update your mindset.

The good news is that many have updated their mindset and

set the destination for their life. They embraced the idea that your mindset can help set your course. Also, they looked at updating the mentality as a journey towards self-fulfillment. You may be sitting there wondering how to get the benefits of visualization too.

So let's take a look at simple ways to improve your ability to visualize. This will include visualization techniques to manifest what you need in your life. This tool is often underlooked, even though it can give you many benefits. Most elite athletes and even executives in their field use this technique to achieve hyperfocus and great results.

The first benefit that I noticed immediately is that it will activate what is within your subconscious mind and will connect your life experiences and education to bring you creative energy for your goal. Also, it has been known to reprogram your brain to understand the stimuli more rapidly and readily look for the resources and tools that are known to help bring your dreams to life. In this way, it will bring forth the law of attraction, which states that your thoughts will always give you the ability to attract the things you want.

You give your best goals focus, and the law of attraction activates this for you. So you can expect to see people and everything you need to make your dreams a reality. This means that it will help you achieve your goals quicker than ever. When you use visualization, there is a change that will take place within you, and that is that your internal will to act becomes more durable, so you will ensure you take action every day so you can meet your goals. There are many benefits to applying visualization in your life, but I'm sure you are more excited about using it.

Let's look at this detail to give you a better idea of how you can start using visualization today. It's such a simple process where you put yourself in a cozy and comfortable setting while also taking time to imagine your best life and result. It has to be visceral and in detail. For example, if you want to be wealthy, give the wealth a number and give it a date you would like to achieve it by. Even if you're going to start a family, then imagine what your family will look like. Think about how many kids you will have and also your husband or wife and think about how this life of yours would look. Make it as though it has already happened for you, and this would be planting the first seed. There is an excellent story of how Jim Carrey, the actor, and comedian, used visualization to earn his first million dollars. He was broke and driving around, and he decided to stop and write himself a check for 30 million dollars. It was not something he could cash, but he chose to believe that his movie career would take off. The truth was that it was soon after it became a reality, and the movie "The Mask" had become a blockbuster earning him 30 million dollars along the way. The power of visualization is certainly something we should consider that has worked countless times in the past. Whether people use visualization to achieve their long term or short term goals, there is merit in its efficacy and how it can help people.

Here are the three techniques you can use that will also help you:

Mental rehearse - this technique is commonly used by

athletes, yet the Russians first used it. During the mental rehearsal, all you need to do is take a few minutes out of your preference early in the morning right after you wake up. Alternatively, you could choose to do it in the evening as well. It needs a peaceful state of mind. The first step is to imagine yourself in a calm and quiet space like the beach or any area that soothes you. While you are in this space, aim to think about your goals and plans for the next day, week, and year and convene with yourself on what you hope to achieve. Make it vivid and bring up all of your hopes and dreams into this particular space. If you do this every day, you will immediately solidify your goals and vision for the future.

Create pictures of your goals - Another way to practice visualization is to make it realistic by taking a picture with your goal. A good example is if you would like to own a particular house, go and view the property and make sure you get a picture of yourself and the property. The idea here is that you are allowing the concept of this property being yours to be embedded within your mind, and this will push you towards achieving that goal.

Write down your goals daily - Written affirmations can be quite powerful in that it connects the thoughts with paper and makes it a reality. Doing this every day keeps this connection going. You may consider writing five goals every day, to begin with, and reviewing them every night before bed.

The processes highlighted are brilliant in allowing you to update your assumptions and beliefs about yourself. They can stimulate your brain cells and get them moving in a purposeful direction and one that you wish to go in. The tools and techniques are useful, but it must also have an excellent environment to thrive in. This usually means ensuring you practice visualization daily and surround yourself with great people who bring positivity and strengths. Couple that with books that give you insight, and you will be golden. In the previous chapter, I discussed how mindfulness and meditation could also be useful in your means to create a vision for yourself for the future. When creating this destination, you wish to get to; it does also help to practice being in the moment, taking things as they come and being present.

Persistence

While visualization is vital to success, and understanding and knowing the techniques I shared will help you - you must be ready for action and failure. It is inevitable on your journey towards reaching your highest self. Thinking about persistence will immediately set your mind to work thinking about grit, resilience, and always going the extra mile in everything you. How many of us have experienced some sort of failure within our lifetime? It is only standard because we are human. Therefore it can be said to be inevitable. If it's unavoidable, we can then become used to the idea that we must prepare for failure. We know it will happen, and we know it will be devastating, so we must prepare ourselves to keep despite the harshest of defeats.

Also, failure is something we can use as a stepping stone. Without faults, there would be no success at all. It is a right of passage to the club of success. If you consider Netflix, an internet company that supplies digital entertainment to over 190 countries and has 185 million subscribers, they also experience failure. They failed to serve their customers and decided to favor a new approach that appeared to be profit-seeking. What did they do? Well, you know that Netflix first started as a DVD delivery service, which put blockbuster out of business. Well, initially, they had two functions, namely Netflix and Qwikster. Qwikster was meant to help deliver DVD's and had a mailing group, and so did Netflix.

However, Netflix decided to create two separate entities and have their subscribers pay for both. Customers were not having it and swiftly canceled their subscription, all 800,000 of them. What did Netflix do? They apologized because they knew it was an error on their part. They learned from their mistake and decided to look into this idea of "binge-watching" DVDs, which people did with the older boxsets. They created a show that they owned and could release in one round that viewers could choose to binge-watch. It worked like a charm and has been their business model ever since. Nowadays, most of their shows are binge-worthy and set the trends for digital content. You can see that Netflix had a failure that could have crippled them, but they chose to view that as a mistake that could be overcome. They persisted and came out with an even better idea, which was the game-changer for them.

The story of Netflix is not an outlier in the business world. Persistence and success also go hand in hand. They are the brother of failure, and they sort of accompany each other to help you achieve your destination. You may be at a stage where you've tried so many times to succeed and are on the verge of quitting, but keep in mind that Thomas Edison invented the commercial light bulb after 1000 iterations. He experimented with so many versions that did not work that he discovered new avenues for it to work along the way. Therefore you get a glimpse into his persistence along the way. While many others would have given up, he decided to keep on going and push forward to bring the electric light bulb to every home. This removed the need for candles and started the path to delivering more appliances to the homefront.

Yet, what could persistence help you with? If you have a current vision that you have in mind, but you still have not achieved it. You could diagnose the situation and find out you quit too soon. If that's the case, it will help immensely even if the feeling of quitting came to mind, but you pushed through anyway and did it one more time. That one last time could lead to the results you want.

Here are the best tips to help you persist amidst challenging circumstances:

Stay in your lane - This usually could mean ignoring everyone else's progress as it's merely a distraction that's not necessarily right. Know that you have your journey to walk while others have theirs. You certainly don't know what they face in their process, and they don't know what's happening with you. Therefore it does not help that you compare yourself with others.

Appreciate little wins - The big wins are phenomenal, but when you have mini-milestones along the way, these can give you the bump of motivation you need to keep you going. The path to self-improvement as an entrepreneur can be daunting, but a little win can go a long way. It could be something small, like getting your website running or updating your social media strategy. These aspects do matter, and they make a difference.

Focus on the next step - If your goals are massive, they can sometimes feel so far away and seem impossible. It's good because it means your goals are worth it, and it will be even better when you achieve that goal. Yet, it can seem so far away, so it's a great idea to set a milestone and focus on taking the next step to propel you forward. You can remind yourself that yes, the main goal exists, but one more step will push you closer. Every action taken is a step that will get you ever closer to where you wish to end up, i.e., your destination.

Know your strengths - Many focus on the areas of improvement and waste time, but I urge you to focus on your strengths and keep growing here. Where your areas of development need work, then do that work but don't dwell on it. Hire people to help with those areas and support you there. It will be worth spending the time and money getting that support. As an example, if you are a big picture thinker and visionary, it may be that detailed orientation is not in your range. You then bring in a partner or team member that is highly detail-oriented and have them focus on those aspects of running your business.

Don't look for an easy way - I'm all for thinking smartly about processes, which can prove helpful and get things done faster. You must use that but also aim to always push through challenges instead of giving up at the first sign of difficulty. Instead, embrace those challenges and make it part of your road to success.

In this section, I wanted to show you that you must have a destination for you to achieve success. In the absence of a target, you don't realize the results or your goals. There are many ways to find your destination, yet my essential tools were centered around visualization and how it can be a quick routine added to your morning or evening. Additionally, I noted that it takes persistence to reach your goals truly.

Therefore now that you understand the fundamentals around having a destination, it does not have to be a daunting task, and you can swiftly start to set your plans in motion. You will then be able to create your destiny in your business instead of thinking of luck.

Key takeaways

Your destination is determined by you and is embedded within your mindset. You have to foster the ideas in your mind to bring you a fruitful goal.

A profitable goal is not enough; you must harness the power of visualization to set yourself into action. This daily reminder of your goal can be done in your mind's eye or through a written means. Writing has been proven to connect your goals physically and steer you in that direction.

To reach your destination, you need a combination of

visualization and persistence. This means it's not enough to visualize simply; it's also necessary to add in action to your process. You must treat failure as a stepping stone to success and use it to fuel your way forward.

Action steps

1. Spend time thinking about your final destination by either visualizing the end goal or writing it down in your journal.
2. Commit to taking an action that will lead you to get closer to what you envisioned and share that action with a close friend or loved one.

CHAPTER 3
Increase productivity

Since the dawn of time, people have pondered this very question of increasing productivity. Their goal was to be better than their fellow humans and to exceed their expectations. Some people tried to be productive by making their bodies ready to do more when work was more manual. You know the age when humans were not quite in the digital age, and work was less cerebral and involved hours of labor outside. Of course, there were always privileged people who employed the people who toiled as laborers.

Then they had the idea that they should increase the productivity of their employees. Let's consider the Ford Motor Company as an example. We know Ford as a maker of quality cars that have been around since 1903. That's quite a long time to be making cars, but you may be surprised that they pioneered some of the productivity elements in the modern workforce. He created a form of incentive where he doubled workers' wages to manufacture cars in his assembly line, which was practically unheard of before.

In doing so, it brought more people to this company, which increased the overall productivity. During this time, Henry

Ford (founder) noticed that people had two types of motivation and that either intrinsic motivation, which is not related to material rewards, or it was extrinsic, which relied on external bonuses, which was related to material rewards like money. Using the outward approach was about using a stick and carrot method to help people become productive. Yet using intrinsic motivation, which was that this motivation could come from your vision and internal to you, he could motivate his employees to do a quality job and increase their productivity.

So, increasing productivity can be achieved by having intrinsic motivation for the work you will do. Motivation can be fueled by looking at your goals and seeing that it matches your highest purpose for yourself, and we also learned that being in control can put you in the driver's seat of your life. Yet, the idea of productivity lies in action taken but depends on your innate motivation. For example, if you have a project that needs to be completed in a week and you are internally motivated by getting the work done because it satisfies you, it will increase your productivity as you would be excited to work on it. Alternatively, if you look at the work as merely a way to attain monetary rewards, you will experience a diminishing sense of reward. It motivated you initially, but the more you achieve that reward, the more it seems like it does not satisfy.

Overall, it helps to have intrinsic motivation in your work, but you cannot always rely on that you have to make systems for yourself to improve productivity. As a business owner, you are faced daily with numerous tasks that need your capacity to think at a high level, but you need to keep a level of consistent productivity without burning out. This means you should work consistently every day without getting complacent and taking the day off as it will mess with your momentum. Intuitively you know that working continuously is a way to increase productivity. The more you do, the more you want to do, and you can also get into a state of flow. The state of flux is where you work at your ultimate potential and achieve up to 300x your usual productivity level.

The question then remains: "How do you keep yourself in a state of flow so you can increase your productivity."

This is the question I'll answer in this chapter and give you the tools that equip you to increase productivity within your day so that you meet and exceed the deadline. Also, it will help you gain all of the opportunities that were previously missed because you were only at 80% productivity level.

Contents

Creating routines
Getting organized

Creating routines

When you think of routines, you may think about a military way of operating, which seems quite taxing. It appears that many leaders suggest routine means that you wake up early at 05 am. It could even mean that you make your bed and have a special breakfast to bring you high performance. Others swear by the idea of meditating in the morning or exercising, while more and more people are adding journaling to their daily practice. This can be seen in people's new way of managing the busy tendencies of modern-day life. Some people opt to hire more people to support their productivity like a virtual assistant or someone who can help them run day-to-day operations.

Others are less fortunate and have to figure out ways to be more productive without spending more money. It can be challenging, but what I have found is that creating a routine for yourself can be the game-changer you need to make the most out of your 24 hours. Since you only have so many hours in your day and there is one you, you must aim to maximize each moment. Some people like to have a morning and evening routine, while others prefer to take a more laissez-faire approach to habits. This means they often do it when they feel the need to. In this section, I will discuss more structured methods to routines, which will center around what you do in the morning (preferably just after you wake up) and your plans in the evening(just before your head to bed).

Studies are also increasingly showing that our habits power our daily actions. This means that the more you do a task, the more opportunity it gets to enter your subconscious mind. Keep in mind that the brain only processes a chore; it inputs into your memory bank, good or bad. So you have to program productive tasks into your mind intentionally. You may have seen the famous quote by Aristotle, which tells us, "We are what we repeatedly do. Excellence, then, is not an act, but a habit." Therefore routines build habits.

Here is how routines can help you:

Prioritize - A good routine will help you see what is essential. The fact that you take time to schedule your day to do a task in a certain way tells your brain what to consider as critical and what not to. Therefore, your routines and habits help you make choices and remove the overthinking aspect of getting work done.

No more distractions - As a busy individual, you know how distractions can curb your flow of productivity. And you also know how easy it is to lose your focus. Yet when you build a routine into your day, you automatically start getting used to the idea that you will know inherently what to do on any given day. It will block out those pesky distractions that creep up from time to time. You could then say that routines make you more self-aware of time stealers and bring you back to what's necessary.

Frees up energy and time - Barack Obama famously said that he wears the same color suit every day so that he did not need to focus on the mundane task of choosing clothing. It took away from his capacity to make crucial decisions. Similarly, Steve Jobs wore the same style of attire because he did like to busy his mind with simple decisions that took him away from the more important ones. These two examples show how routines such as choosing clothing can hinder you. Once you then put it on autopilot, so to speak, you will free up mental space and energy too. You can then use that space and energy to do more.

Say hello to creativity - It seems strange that routine will help you be more creative. It does because having a daily routine will free up your mind so more ideas can enter, and you can leverage the creative mind. The myth that creativity comes from a place far away from routine is simply not true. It is more clear actually that innovative ideas will come from consistency of purpose and giving time to learn your craft.

As you can probably tell, creating your routine and building habits are an excellent way to increase productivity. The foundation of this idea lies in the fact that you are freeing up thinking space and allowing your energy to keep flowing. You may remember a time where you were so mentally exhausted but had not done much work. It may have been due to a stressful time in your life or lack of sleep, yet it caused you to be less productive. But when you added more structure in the form of routines and habits, suddenly, you pushed past your limitation and set your goals higher than ever. Simply the impossible becomes possible.

I'm now going to share routines that can help you. These are ideas and inspiration for you to use as you set forth on self-improvement in your life.

Wake up earlier - I mentioned this before briefly, but I think it's important to understand why waking up early increases your overall productivity. The first part is when you wake up at 4 or 5 am. You are awake while everyone is asleep. The world is still, and you are at your peak level of alertness. You don't have to worry about deadlines looming or emails that need feedback. You also can take your time and work as effectively as possible. Many people also use the extra time to meditate, take a walk or run, write in their journal, or study. You could also add more ideas to the list to try when you wake up earlier. It may be challenging to wake up early at first, especially if you're a late sleeper, but once a week or so has passed, and you commit to doing it daily - you will see it becomes more natural, and you start to look forward to your mornings as well.

Sleep well - Just as important as it is to wake up earlier, also it means you must sleep so that you get 7 hours or more of sleep. Increasingly it's showing that sleep deprivation can be a significant cause for unnecessary accidents at the workplace. So it helps to sleep well and practice excellent sleep health. This means that you should sleep every day at the same time and wake up at the same time. It means you should shut down all technology 2 hours before bed. Also, very important is never to hit that snooze button. I know it's so tempting, but when you keep hitting that snooze button, it tells your brain you want to keep snoozing, which becomes a bad habit. Opt to spring out of bed instead and take a shower, which will immediately set you up for a good day.

Make your bed - TedTalks recently had an excellent talk from an Army Veteran. He told of how in his time in the army, one of the most important lessons he learned was that he should make his bed. He says that the simple task of making your bed in the morning prepares you for the day ahead. It shows that at least one task can be completed successfully and gives you the confidence to face the day. On the upside also he says if you had a bad day, you could always come home to a well-made bed, which you made. Making your bed is helpful and promotes an excellent start to the day, it's a simple habit but one with far-reaching positive effects.

Journal - A simple journal practice will center your focus and teach you what is essential for the day. By writing down your day's happenings, you get to read back what's happening within your mind's depths. You can think about the ideas and observe your thinking, making notes to improve the mindsets that are not getting you anywhere. You may also find that looking back at your journal a couple of years later will make you realize how much progress you made.

Don't check emails - Okay, yes you must check emails as there could be essential tasks needed. But you must aim not to check emails as soon as you wake up. In short, it can be stressful to a mind that is not adequately prepared for the day. A better option would be to schedule time for emails once a day and let others know you will have a 24 hour turnaround time to manage the expectations.

Batching work - Discovering the concept of batching has been a game-changer for me. I always used to think that all tasks should be done in a specific order. Yet when I found out how to batch, I had to switch my framework of how work is completed. For me, the importance of batching lies in how you organize your work and find similar processes. Applying this and finding those processes is merely a matter of time to sit down and do it. For example, if you have emails that need feedback and your mailbox also needs to be checked, set aside time every day to go through all of the emails. Only check your emails once a day, if possible. Another example is where you need to make similar call types and aim to make those on the same as yours to be more prone to be effortless and service-oriented.

Apply GTD principles - This stands for Getting Things Done. It's a framework created by David Allen, who noticed that people were so scattered. He observed that the brain was supposed to be used for thinking and not storing stuff. His system relies on decluttering your mind and prioritizing all tasks in a system like your inbox or Trello. This has worked brilliantly for so many people who needed to think creatively to be more productive. The principles are also available in a book, and you can check out the official website for all the content you need.

Take a break - With so many things to take care of in your busy day, you may think that working all the time will make you more productive. It does the opposite and could lead to burnout. Use the time to take a break and get into a hobby. For example, if you love to hike, then take time out to do that and come back refreshed, you will be 10x more productive upon your return.

Routines are a great way to start reframing how you work. Some people hire staff to support their productivity, but when you don't have that luxury, you must think of ways to reduce time on tasks. You do this by making your daily routine with minimal complications. It's a way to plan your life and bring structure to your day. You can have a morning, evening, or all-day routine. The most important part of having a routine is that it suits you. There's no use having a fancy routine if you do not follow it. I urge you to start small and work yourself up to more significant routines and habits over time. These will stick and will be much more enjoyable for you in the long run. You will turn out to be more productive and consistent.

Even if routines make you more productive, they cannot always be used for every challenge you have. Therefore, it's essential to explore other options to help you stay productive. The next option I want us to consider is how you stay organized for the maximum benefit.

Maybe you are like me, where the organization reminds me of the girl in 7th grade who always color-coded her notes and had the most organized files. She made the best notes and also always looked so well put together and never rattled by anything. Yet, there are many ways we can borrow from that level of organization that also makes a person productive. That same 7th-grade girl even went to every club you could imagine while also taking advanced language courses after school. She managed something that few others get to do, she stayed productive amidst busy periods in her life.

Getting organized

The truth is that people who are organized were not born that way. They found a way to become organized and learned from others who showed this skill. So even if you are someone who is not very organized, you can quickly learn this skill. It could help you plan, keep notes, and remove clutter from your life.

If you're willing to learn and take action, then you will quickly become an organization maestro. Also, practice is essential, and knowing that you will fail the first few times, but you have to keep going. As they say, practice makes perfect when learning new skills. Every pro was once a beginner, so take heart in this fact and look at how you can learn the ropes of organizing your life one step at a time.

These are some of my findings after observing hundreds of organized individuals.

Write things down - we discussed the power of writing previously, but getting organized is often a matter of taking aspects that are scattered in your brain and turning it into a list. This could be a daily to-do list or goals for your week/year/month. We all know someone who remembers every person's birthday or anniversary. It's not some secret magic they possess; it's more like they have found ways to write and keep things in an ordered way. Nowadays, you don't only have to use a pen and paper, but digital tools in the palm of your hand can work just as well.

Apps such as Todoist and Trello are great organization tools. Or simply use your notes app on your phone. As is true, the head should be used for thinking and not storing stuff, so don't try and complicate your life by memorizing dates, reminders - use technology to your advantage and set these on your phone. Ensure you get everything down, such as a list for shopping, gifts, and important dates. You could even take it a step further and get into the habit of writing people's names down; this will help you build your networking muscles.

Create schedules - You probably dislike schedules as much as the next person, but it can help you manage your time. People often infringe on others' time, but with a schedule, you will always be on the clock and have something planned. You can often schedule tasks in your calendar and then use that as a reminder to finish that task. In reality, you will find that by creating schedules, you don't feel the need to waste time anymore, knowing it is so precious. Living a lifestyle filled with clutter, and no schedules mean there isn't time and clarity for your goals.

Delegate - Most people love to hoard their work when others can do it better. It could be fear of loss of control or hurt in the past due to failed delegation. That does not mean it cannot work. Delegation is vital if you run a business or work in management as it's the only way to get a hold of all of your work. Yet delegation is about getting the best people to work on tasks and playing to your strengths.
Furthermore, it's about growing your team and strengthening them for a new promotion in the future. Many people also use freelancers to delegate their workload. They will often seek out a virtual assistant to help keep control of their calendar or other critical engagements.

Declutter - A cluttered home or office generally means a cluttered mind, and that leaves less room for you to do more and be productive. Seek to find items that have no use and give them away or throw them out. Don't buy the stuff you do not need, as this only serves to create clutter for you. Organize your home and desk every week for the best results. Finally, create a space where you keep stuff after a long day at work. It could mean a bowl on the kitchen table where all loose coins and other stuff go. Then take time to declutter that bowl. At least you know there is one spot for clutter instead of everywhere.

Overall, you can see that getting organized can be so satisfying as it takes away the mental clutter you may have. It frees your mind up to do more in a day and be more productive with the time you do have.

In this section, I wanted to show you practical ways to become more productive over a short period swiftly. You had the chance to learn how to create routines that stick and improve productivity. While also learning all about getting organized and staying that way.

Key takeaways

When you think about increasing your productivity, there is always an underlying challenge at play. That relates to the current state of your habits and routines. Additionally, it may merely be a symptom of a lack of organization at present.

If you are not productive at present, it can always be fixed. You can make a concerted effort to add more good habits into your routine while slowly removing the bad ones.

Furthermore, it does help create routines that will save you time and energy and are more on autopilot.

Getting organized is another way to be productive. There are countless ways to get organized, and most involve writing down your task, decluttering, delegating, and creating schedules.

Action steps

1. Spend a day in your week, reflecting on the work you have done and rate yourself on a scale of 1-5 on how productive you have been. If you have a 5, it means you finished all tasks on your to-do-list. If lower, then it could use some work, and that could be your focus area.
2. Start a morning routine by choosing three things you must do in the morning. It could be as simple as waking up at 05 am, drinking coffee, and reading.
3. Reflect on your organization skills, and ask your colleagues or family members how they think you can improve.

CHAPTER 4
Invest in interpersonal skills

If you work in a space requiring two or more people to be in one area, then you create room for the concept of interpersonal skills to operate. Some people have excellent interpersonal skills, while others do not. Yet it's a skill, and therefore you can learn to improve if it's not your strong suit.

But what exactly are interpersonal skills?

These skills are the ones we use daily when talking to others in a personal or professional context. Often it shows up in group settings but can be just as prominent in individual setups too. There are many skills under the umbrella of interpersonal skills, but one that stands out and is most commonly referred to is how people listen and speak to each other effectively. There is also an element of emotional intelligence involved in interpersonal skills. This means how people manage their feelings and emotions when conversing with each other.

If you've worked in an office, it's common to see many opposing viewpoints and personalities. Some people are loud, obnoxious, and bullish, while others are more passive, sensitive, and, at times, even manipulative. Yet this is the nature of working in a space filled with people who have a variety of personalities. It's a reality that every person is unique as they have their feelings, beliefs, upbringings, and experiences, and they use this to show up in conversations. For example, you may have an employee who always seems to be gloomy and sullen while you have another jovial, upbeat, and a bit too much. If they are in the same team, they can quickly start to create tension if neither has interpersonal skills to manage conflict situations.

Conflict situations are everyday occurrences and can range from mild dislike to full blow physical fights on a spectrum. As a rule, most companies ensure they have values that govern how people must behave so that most people will follow these. Yet, inherently there are a few that will act on feeling and emotion, which will result in unnecessary insult and friction in the workplace. So the only way to handle such situations is to invest in your interpersonal skills so that whoever you engage with will always come out with a win-win situation—one where each party leaves the interactions feeling empowered and with warm feelings towards the other.

Contents

Going for mutual benefits
Listening to understand
Maximizing the combined efforts

Going for mutual benefits

Inherently, we always want to have a win-win situation in our dealings with people. This is generally the case. The idea of pulling the wool over another person's eyes seems downright unimpressive, and yes, there may be a few who would get excitement and joy from this action, but most people will not. Therefore the idea of going in for mutual benefits is about getting a win-win situation. What does this mean? It was first popularised by Steven Covey, who wrote the seven habits of highly effective people. In the later chapters in his books, he shares that you also gain the respect of people you interact with when you aim to get a mutual benefit. Now only do they trust you more, but your reputation grows with other leaders and teams in your organization.

There are many ways to go for mutual benefit, and it may take longer than having a simple win-lose situation, but the time is worth the relationship. When you enter a win-win position, you say that you value the person enough to engage and take time to conclude. In organizations today, it's challenging to find people who will take time with relationships not because they intend to but because it is so busy. So the win-win concept becomes even more critical, and finding ways for employees to have more time to implement this strategy is vital.

If you are currently a business owner who has many people on their team, you may want to consider how your team is doing from this aspect. Culture can be broken so quickly, and that can damage productivity. You want the win-win concept to flow through your organization and improve it. Even if you do diagnose that the strategy is not at play, it's never too late to update it.

Listening to understand

The trend has surfaced recently, where conversations are monopolized by people who set out to listen without considering what people are saying. They use it as opportunities to express their agenda. For example, you may be receiving valuable feedback about your business. Still, if you are waiting to get your work done, you miss this information and miss out on building a good working relationship. Listening to understand then becomes essential to any business owner.

Taking the time to listen actively instead of passively is a skill. It's a skill that can be learned and used for good. When you listen actively, you are present in the conversation and focus on the person. You aim to make them comfortable so that they can give you the information without fear or judgment. Also, you will intend to ask questions as and when necessary to support them. If you are a coach, it is an excellent way to bring out limiting beliefs, challenge them gently, and help the people you speak to.

You may find that the more you listen to understand, the more people will enjoy their time spent with you. They will find ways to stay in touch by engaging over social networks like LinkedIn and Facebook, and they introduce you to others in their network. It's also about providing value to people you engage with. You want to deliver value, so they can see you want to help them even if you are not paid for that work. In time, you will know that you will grow your brand and reputation extensively just by listening to people.

Maximizing the combined efforts

Teamwork can surely make the dream work, but how can it maximize your outputs. Let's find out in this section. If you've ever worked in a team, you know that people come in all shapes, sizes, and opinions. It is a challenge to expect people to be just like you simply. So you need to embrace the differences of the people you work with. The world of work has changed significantly where it used to be that work culture was quite hierarchical, and so too many leaders were applauded for the autocratic style of leadership. People expected that life at work would be a challenge and braced themselves for it. Times have changed; the workforce has updated, and guess what? People want collaboration, and they want diversity in approaches, and leaders need to follow along with this concept.

Therefore, the new leader has evolved into a transformational leader who does not focus on the status quo. The focus has shifted to collaboration and using their interpersonal skills to grow relationships. In organizations, the value of social relationships can mean the difference between your project moving forward or being sidelined. Understandably, you may not be the type of person with excellent interpersonal skills, so how do you then learn to compensate for those skills? By working together with others who can help you build those skills. At first, it might prove to be a challenge, but the more you add effort and keep practicing, you will see an improvement in your skillset.

This will become a tool that you can then use in your work

and life going forward. People value interpersonal skills, and in recent studies, employees talk about the concept of emotional intelligence, which is known as your EQ. Their findings show that when two candidates have a similar intelligence quotient, they most often look at the emotional intelligence of a person to determine their fit for the job. Emotional intelligence looks at self-awareness as in how you can observe yourself and make changes to behaviors. Still, also it looks at your social awareness and how you engage with people. The idea being that since teamwork is the norm, then employees need to use these skills to get along and build a conducive environment for optimal performance.

Key takeaways

Investing in interpersonal relationships gives you soft power. This is a power that does not use aggression or violence. Instead, it uses communication skills to aid the link. It supports a growing personal and professional relationship, which will help you network in the future.

When you commit to interpersonal relationship knowledge, you say that you wish to go for mutual benefits in a working relationship. You also bring across the idea that you should try to understand the people you work with and know what they may be facing in their world. Further, it also looks at making teamwork, work.

Listening to understand is always about the other person and how you make them feel. People will warm to you when you make an effort to understand them and add value to their life. If you listen to respond, then you will win very little favor amongst people.

Teamwork is the only way to achieve more than you thought you could. It's one way of maximizing the combined benefits of a talented group of people working together. It will surprise you what could be achieved when people know trust and collaborate. It would help if you leveraged this when seeking to improve your interpersonal skills.

Action steps

1. Commit to watching one video or learning resource on growing your interpersonal skills. Then when you have an opportunity to practice, use it, and notice how it changes the way people relate to you. Rinse and repeat.
2. Always aim for a win-win situation in every interaction, put yourself in others' shoes, and create space for getting that win. Cultivate this by finding ways to compromise in your home life, and then slowly moving this into the work context.
3. Work in a team as much as possible. The next time a project comes along, be the first person to volunteer to lead the project and gather a team to work on it.

CHAPTER 5
Continuous Improvement

If I had to ask you, what does continuous improvement mean to you? What would you say? Would you choose to tell me that growth was about perfection? Or would you say progress? Improvement itself is a concept that has been with us for centuries, where the human spirit is such that it seeks to get better, to improve on the last version of a task. This, in itself, is something that is not new. Therefore improvement becomes a state of doing better at different milestones. You may find that you have a journey of a thousand miles, but when you consider it, then a thousand miles seems so much. You must take a step back and know that you move forward in stages. Every moment, every stage and every opportunity is there for you to make incremental growth. Consider, for a moment, the athlete who is at the top of their game. They did not merely end up that way by chance; it was through practice. As a kid, they may have had a dream.

This dream was incorporated in how they lived their lives from that day onwards. Now, if their parents supported that dream, they would have been their biggest fans. They would have admitted them to the best athletics programs and made sure that they had a good home life. Even so, it was always on the kid to keep practicing, waking up early and training. They had to skip hanging out with friends, and going to all fun activities. They always had to make the choice to get better or do the most comfortable thing. In this choice, they could choose the path of least resistance where they would have fun or where they needed to put effort, hard work, and be patient. Training, preparing, and practicing is hard. It makes you more resilient and helps your mind think in unexpected ways. You start to see that practice and improvement go hand in hand. There can be no improvement without training. People often talk about famous athletes like basketball player Micheal Jordan who is known to have some of the most phenomenal stats. Initially, when he started playing at school, his coach would say he could not play a specific position in the game, and for him, that was a motivator. He saw it as a chance to prove the coach wrong, and after practicing, preparing, he improved, and the coach was impressed.

Even later on, he was consistently trying to beat his last high score during his professional days of basketball. He became good at offense and defense, and when he was not suitably skilled at a shot, he would spend many hours and days mastering those skills. He was committed to doing better, getting better and growing. This is the essence of this chapter, where I want to show you that improvement is possible, and necessary if you wish to become the entrepreneur of your life. If you're going to thrive in almost every iteration of life, you have to reform yourself, learn, grow, and repeat.

Contents

Practicing Temperance
Getting rid of bad habits
Seeking Discomfort

Reading Often

Think about the last book you read? It could be via an
audiobook, Kindle, or paperback. If you think about that
book, imagine your favorite aspect and how it made you feel.
If it made you feel inspired, you could see how reading can be
somewhat beneficial. If it made you take action, you could see
that reading played a role in moving forward with plans. If
you did not finish, then perhaps a reframe of the reason is
needed. All in all, you can see that reading is a profoundly
personal fact in your life. Bill Gates, the founder of Microsoft
and technology magnate, recently did an interview, and he
shared that he gets through 50 books a year. That's roughly
four books a month.

He reads mostly nonfiction, business books where he
introduced us to books like Outliers, Sapiens and Headspace.
These are good books, and not only do they help you ignite
your brain and make better connections, but they also serve to
give you new insight and ways of viewing the world. These
books offer research that is shared in a creative and thought-
provoking manner. The authors have sometimes spent
decades reading and collating information to help you make
sense of the world. You can then access this knowledge easily
by buying a book for less than 3 cups of coffee at Starbucks. If
that's not a great situation, then you may as well find free
versions of books. You can find   many book repositories

online that offer free classic books like Openlibrary and Gutenberg.

Even more than that, you can invest in a kindle unlimited membership and read for free. It works like a library where you can loan out books for a set amount of time and read it. Once done, you can return the book and take out another. The books are free because you pay a monthly subscription that allows you access to the world's best books like wealth books, finance books, and mindset management books.

You may be wondering, but where do I find the time to read so many books. If you have a smartphone, you are already very fortunate because when you get a book, you can have it on your phone and read it wherever you go. Let's say you're on the bus, and there is traffic then on your ride home you can plug in your headphones, and take the next 20-25 minutes to read 15 pages or more. If you read 15 pages every day for a month, you would have read two medium-sized books.

How else can you find the time? How about if you gym daily, and for 20 minutes you're on the treadmill, you can quickly use audiobooks and listen while you exercise. The concept of multi-tasking has never been better. As you can tell, reading can be done rapidly and over time. The benefits are immense, where one study shows us that reading can expand your memory bank, increases your ability to connect the dots, and can even make you more creative.

Practicing Temperance

The concept of a temper originates from the idea that a

person's state of mind is seen in terms of their being angry or calm. A person can be either, and this can impact their entire day. If you choose to be calm in the face of challenges, then your day is better. If you choose anger, you may find yourself becoming someone who ruins others' days.

You build a habit of being temperamental where people do not know what to expect from you, even how to approach you. In this way, you must cultivate a space where you can practice temperance. Temperance is one of the virtues notes in cultural texts, which says moderate their behavior so that they do not indulge too much in activities that will harm them. This could be in partaking too much in alcohol or in procrastinating and playing PC games instead of doing the work that needs to be done to succeed. Think of it as the idea of moderation in practicing self-control.

We do all have guilty pleasures, which make us enthusiastic about what it may bring. Yet if we lived in that state all the time, those pleasures become less pleasurable. Some people may find that they love to sleep for 10 hours or more, but as a human being, you only need 6-7 hours of sleep. When you overindulge, it can be bad for your health. When you practice temperance, you have the insight to know that you must do everything in moderation or abstain from it. This is especially true if you have not yet built the habit of self-control, or delaying gratification.

A study was done years ago, where researchers decided to do an experiment where they told kids that there were many marshmallows, and if they could delay eating the marshmallow and have it later, they would get three marshmallows.

The kids all reacted differently; some kids did not even try and went straight for the marshmallow. Others tried their best not to look at it, and some also had physical turmoil trying not to touch and eat the marshmallow. Over their life, the studies followed them, showed that those who did not choose to take the marshmallow and showed restraint often did the same in later life, leading them to be more successful in the studies and their work life. The same process is happening in your head daily where you have two options, one to delay gratification for a later reward and another to simply follow your feelings. If you choose to follow your feelings, you may feel happy at that moment but will regret it later by thinking: "I wish I could have studied more instead of hanging with my friends." or "I will put more effort into that project instead of messing around at work."

The good news is that you can cultivate a sense of temperance if you previously did not have it. Our personalities are not fixed, although it may be challenging to change. If you can be committed to improving your self-control, then you will have the never to make it happen. Your goal will drive you on, knowing what a difference practicing temperance makes versus not practicing it. The question then becomes: How do you go about building the temperance muscle? There are many ideas in the best way, so let me share a few practical and can be easily applied.

Analyze your life - Usually, this would mean taking stock of what has transpired in your life and what you thought was right and what was not. It's doing an audit, to know where you have lacked the self-control on your goals. You can easily do it by looking back at the roles you've done before and seeing how your lack of self-control or rigor failed you. Take note of these and use them.

Look at where you lack self-control - Once you have compiled a list of the areas you lack self-control in, you now have a working task list to get better. From here, you can see which areas impact you, such as perhaps you tend to procrastinate or indulge in certain activities too much, and this can take away time from getting your work done. Look closely as to what could be the root cause of these issues and work to fix them. While you were reading, you may have discovered tools to guide you, try to apply each of these, and monitor the progress made.

Set your goals so you can reach them - Many people think they have to set goals which are towering and can sometimes be demotivating. It works just as well when you set mini-goals towards your big goals and feel a sense of achievement that will motivate you to keep going. The little milestones count too.

Accountability - Perhaps you work best when you have people who can take you to task if you have not done something you said you would do. In this way, seek these people out and share your plans. It's okay if they are friends or a mentor who will seek to be upfront with you where you have messed up. Alternatively, making your plan public can be a lifesaver, where you share it on social media, which makes you feel more committed to improving. We are generally predisposed to worrying about what others think of us, and it can be a motivating factor when you want people to know you've succeeded.

Review progress - This step is often overlooked, and is one of the most important, where your progress reviews along the way can show you where you may have fallen short, or where you've done well. In instances where you have done well, you can learn from that and apply them in other areas. Also, don't be afraid to look at the failures as these are learning areas that will only make things better if you choose to learn.

Seek help - This can be in improving your knowledge about self-control, or having someone to talk about the challenges you face. The idea of having a support system in place is not a new one. All business owners have a group of people they turn to when things seem a little murky in their companies. These are people who care about you and want to see you succeed. When you can engage in the matter, it might be that you lift a huge weight off your shoulder. This is helpful, and you should aim to go out there and get some help if you need it.

Practicing temperance can make a difference when you aim to be an improved version of yourself. When you decide to bring in more self-control into your life, it's a habit that becomes addictive, and you keep trying to stick to it. It becomes much easier to say no to going out on a Sunday before work, and also you choose to do your assignments or project tasks instead of watching the latest Netflix show. You always aim to choose the right thing for your situation. This is such an essential aspect of improving, which will keep you on the chosen path. Some so many people have overcome severe issues, addictions, and bad habits by merely practicing temperance. Know that it will not always be comfortable, and you will fail from time to time where you will even want to give up. That is simply part of the process. If you stick with it, you see massive gains in the future.

Getting rid of bad habits

In his iconic book, Atomic Habits, James Clear tells us that you can improve your practices and replace those that are derailing your success. His approach is one where you incrementally take on a new pattern that will seek to dislodge the old. Some habits are easy to break, especially if you are not committed to them. Other habits have been with you from a young age that it becomes part of your psyche and how you identify.

These habits have attached themselves to every fiber of your being, and you would feel lost without them. Yet, if the habits are unhealthy like smoking excessively, overindulging in drink, it might be a signal to slow things down and curb those habits. When you have a bad habit, it can take over your life and stop you from reaching your goals. You feel demoralized, unmotivated and it also wastes your energy, making you unwell.

Before we head into solution territory, let's understand how habits form. If you're a graduate student, it might be that you have project work that is often due. If the problem is challenging, and you feel like you cannot do it, there is a push to remove that sense of annoyance, frustration, and even insecurity. What do you do? Immediately the next best thing is to use your phone and check what's happening on Facebook or Instagram. You get a hit of dopamine, which makes you happy, and you feel a sense of relief, but your work is still waiting for you, and it's now also delayed. If this happens every time you find a challenging task, you reinforce checking your phone instead of working.

Another one is when you wake up early but feel less awake than you would like to, so you know the only way is to grab a coffee. You then associated waking up and coffee. Coffee is not necessarily a bad habit, but too much coffee can be overstimulating and be bad for you.

Let's think of what else could be a bad habit that might be keeping you away from self-improvement. Perhaps you love sweet snacks, and every time you feel a sense of stress, you gravitate to the nearest snack. You know it's filled with sugar, but you simply cannot keep yourself away. There might be something that is triggering you. This usually means that you have a feeling that is pushing you towards that snack. In this instance, the root of the issue could lie with your stress levels, and if you had to moderate it, you would be less likely to reach out for the nearest snack. Primarily, you would curb a dangerous habit that affects your health.

Understanding your bad habits are essential. Even more, essential is knowing how to remove them from your life so you can live in a way that is in accordance with your highest calling. You know that stress or boredom can create bad habits, so the underlying triggers of pressure must be dealt with or limited. Some habits are there with you. Maybe it makes you feel better as it is with drugs or alcohol but is harmful to you. Perhaps it is such that it eases your discomfort at the moment as in when you bite your nails or tap your foot, or you have a fear of failure, so you simply choose some other activity instead. Whatever it might be, the trick is in choosing to replace those bad habits in favor of a better life, a better way of operating. For example, if you're someone who wakes up and the first thing you do when you get into the office is checking email, which instantly puts you in a non-productive mood, and can ruin your day. You have to think of how you can replace that habit, and that could be replacing it with something like completing a quick task, which makes you feel confident.

Let's take a look at a process that will work for you to fix bad habits.

What's your alternative - Many habits can easily be removed by replacement. This simply means you find an alternative thing to do in place of your bad habit. Think about the future of a situation, if you are prone to go for a smoke break after a rather nasty work task, then opt to use that sensation to stay at your desk and breathe before going outside. If you are prone to log into social media on your desktop, choose to remove that from your PC by adding a social media blocker during a specific time. Find things to do that help your state of mind, such as instead buying a coke, choose water instead of your meal. The first few times will be challenging as the urge to say yes to a sugary drink will be high, the more you choose water, the better and more durable the good habits get.

Get a buddy - Why go towards a great big goal alone. If

you're on the path to eating well, find someone walking the same and join forces. You will have the same challenges, and having a support structure in place will serve to help you immensely. When times get difficult, you have someone to call, and also you can compare how your diets are going with each, understanding the pain of temptation fully. This reinforcing buddy system will help you immensely and will give you the strength to keep going.

Look for triggers - As discussed earlier in this chapter, a trigger is something that will activate your bad habit. Often your triggers go unnoticed, as you have not taken the time out to be self-aware of your behavior. If, for example, you always choose the same types of sugary snacks without pausing, it may be that you are not aware that you have an issue. If you are not mindful, you won't know what was triggering you. It seems complex at first, but all it means is that there is a feeling behind you wanting that doughnut, or choosing to go for another smoke break. Often it's in the emotion of insecurity, fear, and other negative feelings you wish to get away from. Bad habits act as the bandaids to the senses. It may soothe you at the moment, but the feeling will always resurface. Therefore, you must actively seek out your triggers and work to reduce it and plan for when it will arise. For example, if you are emotional, the shopper makes a rule that you must always take a loved one with you who will bring a list, so you only stick to that list. They will also keep you in check when you are shopping.

Like-minded people - Every person has a group or tribe of people who they naturally gravitate towards. These are the people who have similar positive and nurturing mindsets who are successful. When you are with these people, you are filled with ideas, and you become more enthusiastic about what the world will bring you. People who are not your tribe create friction for you; everything seems like a chore as it's more complicated than anticipated around these people. They simply drain your energy.

You want to move away from that quickly and towards a tribe who is about growing together, but who also provides feedback, shares success, and works through problems together. If you have not found these people, just yet keep on looking around. The online space has made our world a smaller and more connected environment. If you need to find people who fit your tribe, then there online sites like Meetup and Facebook groups that allow like-minded people to congregate and share ideas. Other places in forums like Reddit or business forums.

Use visualization - A visualization is a powerful tool that you have access to. It's the ability to see a better future for yourself. It could be the image or moving picture in your mind's eye that you wake up daily at 05 am and take a run. It could also be the salad you have for lunch or even look at giving a presentation and doing a fantastic job every time. The trick is to make it visceral, feel the sensations, and imagine it as if it was real and let your emotions of excitement and enthusiasm get captured along with it. Soon this visualization will get imprinted into your mind

Don't berate yourself - It happens when things will not always go to plan as you are changing your habits. I urge you to treat yourself with kindness and make it a priority to think of how far you've come. Saying terrible things to yourself is not helpful, but having empathy for your actions and the effort you put in can be extremely helpful. Make it a priority to review your week of habit reformation and think about the progress you made, and say kind words to yourself, such as "you've come further than last week," or "your work ethic is amazing." These simple ideas can mean a world of difference.

Plan, and plan some more: When you change your habits, you're fundamentally changing your biology. It's a hard enough job, so you must be the master of your change. To do this, planning is essential and will be the thing that helps you keep going. Planning means that you plan for roadblocks like challenges and stressors. It means that you allow for failure and don't hold yourself to an unhealthy standard. Planning could also mean that you budget effectively, so you don't have financial stress. Additionally, it will mean you choose to eat well, so you are productive, mentally, and physically. It could also show up within your relationship where you discuss your changes with your loved ones and let them know you are on this journey and need their help.

Following this process may be challenging at first, but if you opt to be diligent and follow through small actions, the more significant steps get more effortless. You become someone who has confidence in their ability, and other people also see this change in you and want to know what's your secret. Your habits took many years to form and will not be removed overnight, have the patience to keep on going even when it seems daunting. I can assure you on the other side of breaking those bad habits; you will be the authentic you who becomes one who seeks discomfort.

Seeking Discomfort

If you are on YouTube looking for educational videos that will help you improve, then a good channel will pop up called "seeking discomfort." The main thing about this channel is that they look to do the extraordinary. They want to do something that makes them feel like they are out of their comfort zone. One such example is that they challenged Will Smith to a dangerous Bungy for his 50th birthday, and he agreed to do it.

The idea that they found a way to meet their idol and movie star led to them doing this impossible jump is one way where they were seeking uncomfortable scenarios, which led to successful ones. For example, the exposure they achieved on their channel was phenomenal as more people were curious to find out about this dare and that Will Smith would be doing it. More people also wanted to know about these guys who had dared Will Smith. The curiosity brought them more fans and gave them notoriety all over the world. It pays to seek discomfort, and later on, one of the group members was invited to one of Will Smith's movies to be an extra. It all started with the idea of seeking discomfort and grew.

So let me ask you this question: How can you leverage this principle of seeking discomfort in your own life? If you said that you could start by finding areas where you are too comfortable, and make plans to step a foot out of the comfort zone. This could be one opportunity.

Begin with the smallest steps, which soon will turn into more significant steps forward. As an example, if you have graduated from college and started working, but you always wanted to further your studies. Each year you put it off because it would make your budget and family life more challenging to manage. What if you decided to start by applying and see what happens. If you apply, you could get accepted, and that makes it more real. Soon, you would have created a visual in your mind of registering for one course, and then before you know it, you would be paying the fees and studying. It starts by taking the first step. Even the future of the first step might bring discomfort to you.

Seeking discomfort is about choosing to move deliberately to the point that is not predictable and disrupts your current situation, but the rewards will be exponential for you.

Key Takeaways

Reading often is one of the habits that if you cultivate it now, it will pay dividends in years to come. You can think of reading as your gateway into a new world where you are offered the secrets of the universe through the pages of books. Almost everyone who has come before we have a story to tell. Their stories are inspiring and shocking, and also they show that people who read are continually improving through the wisdom of other people's lessons. If you choose to read, you want to learn, and that will lead to you cultivating a sense of curiosity.

Practicing temperance often comes to mind when we think about your emotions and feelings. If you are always going to react in an explosive manner to situations, you'll find that life will keep you down. If you get feedback, you will feel like you have been knocked out. So you have to manage your emotions by understanding it. It's more important to know yourself well than to try to change everything about yourself. When you know what you're working with, you are more likely to use it to your advantage in the best way possible.

Getting rid of bad habits will serve to finally clean up those habits that have derailed your progress for the last few years. You know you want to change, but it can be challenging. A habit can be good or bad, but you must always work towards eliminating those bad habits in favor of improved ones. The human spirit craves to be the best version of itself, and you are not any different.

Seeking discomfort is often about pushing your limits. If you always stay complacent and not willing to grow, you will never find your true calling. If you often remain in a place of comfort too scared to move, others will take over you, and you will always live in regret. The essence of seeking discomfort is pushing yourself out of moments where life is too easy. You want to look for the moments which challenge you and make you feel a slight pain level. It means you're growing.

Actions steps

1. When you wake up, make it one of your priorities to read at least ten pages of a business book. If you have it on your

phone, it becomes much easier than scrolling social media.

2. Seek to add temperance as a goal within your life, where you remove toxic habits from your life. Replace these habits with good ones little by little. Have a journal where you note down your progress towards temperance.

3. Do one thing that scares you every week. It could be talking to strangers, or finally, bungee jumping. Make it a challenge for yourself, and if possible, bring a friend along.

As you embark on your continuous improvement journey, you may wonder when the journey will end, and you can take a break. In my experience, the passage of growth and improvement never ends. If you decide to take a break for an extended period, you lose out on the momentum you have already created. You also lose out on the feeling of "flow," which means you are in your highest state of productivity. Studies are even showing us that when you continuously improve, you awaken your sense of intrinsic motivation. This tells you that you do not need rewards externally to feel happy and excited about life. All you need is the feeling inside of progress and doing well. I'd like you to feel encouraged by the opportunity to excel in your life. This is something only humans can do, and which brings a sense of joy. In the next chapter, we'll take it a step further and move from continuous progress to showing you how you can keep on progressing in life and building yourself for a better future.

CHAPTER 6
Progress and Build Yourself

In the last few chapters, my focus has been on helping you grow your ability to take control of your life and find ways also to become more productive. At the heart of this text is the idea that you are the entrepreneur of your life. You hold the key to make changes at every step. Now that you have insight into taking control, it's time to look into how you keep progressing. Our previous focus has been in gearing you up and getting your mindset ready for the immense changes that you will face on your path to entrepreneurial endeavors. This is essentially where the magic happens and how you start to see all the work you applied in the previous sections to pay off. What is progressing about, and how does it help you build yourself?

Let's take a moment to understand the concept of progress first. It is defined as a forward-focused or onward movement toward a destination. Your destination could be a new promotion, or getting into graduate school or finally making a profit in your business. Or your goal could be to travel the world and live a life of adventure. Whatever that destination might be, you will need to make sense of progress towards that goal. You will have to build yourself up to such a point that growth becomes inevitable for you. This type of growth is created by a formula knowing that when you keep consistent, have a force for discipline, and continue reading and learning, you will progress slowly at first. You will start to gain more momentum as the wheel of your plans get into motion, and you begin to give your business the work ethic it needs.

You start to think differently and know that there is an investment that goes into self-improvement. This investment begins with you and how you keep going in the right direction. Many entrepreneurs have faced the daunting task of keeping themselves and their business consistent. It could be that you were just starting and burned the midnight oil to get your business going, but that soon becomes less sustainable. What needs to happen? You have to find a system that agrees with you, and that helps you keep making progress as a consistent approach to your life. Often when you do things erratically, you get inconsistent results, and the pace is also erratic.

This will show up in some days of 12-15 hour work, and on other days you only 1-2 hours. This cannot work as you're training your body and mindset to be inconsistent based on your work ethic. You cannot make progress when your consistency graph looks like a rollercoaster. The reality is that success will come from choosing to have a consistent daily habit and sticking to it. That will be the main focus of this chapter, and also I'll give you the main tools you can use to cultivate consistency in your life and business. Once you have a sense of consistency and the practical tools to create this for your life, we'll move over to how reading can improve your consistency too, when you choose to read from leaders and business owners who have left a mark in this world. Finally, I will show you how important it is to keep looking forward to the next stage and how that can inspire the actions you take today.

Contents

Keep consistent

After working with many students, executives, and business owners, I often find a trend that accompanies their lack of consistency. Many have said it is the fact that as humans, we cannot manage our emotions appropriately, which would push into our lives. The idea that every time life was going well, and they were being productive was often derailed by events that caused havoc to their emotional state.

This could be that they had a challenging relationship with their manager, who did not suit their personality. Often this is a micromanager who turned into become a demoralizing person who made them dislike their work. The employee was unhappy and did not know how to deal with their work. So, they eventually ended up doing the bare minimum at work or did not do work consistently tending to feel demotivated and opting to surf the internet instead of when their manager was not looking. This is one example where one's emotional state can be affected and how that affects your ability to do work consistently.

Let's consider the area where a student is just entering university, and this is their first time experiencing such a heavy workload. Perhaps they thought it would be exactly like their time in school, which had a great support structure and was easy to cope with. In university, you are left to fend for yourself, and figure out your timetable while also being completely new. The first few months are the most important for establishing good habits and a routine. If you fail to get this right, you could end up feeling so overwhelmed that you don't focus or study and eventually cannot keep up with the world. The worst-case scenario is you end up failing. Yet, the university is all about consistency, so we can see that not getting consistency will not serve you.

If you've ever been in a supervisor position, you will know that your performance and the work you do depend on the people you manage. It is hard to be consistent when there are so many people who threaten that state with their multitude of challenges. For example, an employee may have issues at home that impacts their ability to focus at work. Alternatively, another may not be equipped to deal with the job, and is continually putting in extra hours but cannot get it right. These emotional factors will essentially become your problems, as you have to navigate; this will help them meet the company requirements. Mostly you have to keep your emotions in check and help others do the same.

That's where the strategies for consistency can play a role.

Let's look into them below.

Good routine - How you spend the first few moments of your day will represent how your day will go. It will determine if you are flustered when you enter the office and how you manage your workload. When you have a good morning routine, it can help center you and help you get in the right frame of mind. The morning routine can be a simple wake up, shower, eat breakfast, and write in my journal, or it can be more complex where you have ten items on your list. Your routine is all about how you create your day and the things that bring joy into your morning. It's your first few moments of the day, and you have to experience it as pleasurable so you can look forward to what's to come. Athletes are prone to live like this, where they have a routine every time they start their event. Some will close their eyes and visualize, others will mediate, or some will simply read. It's a very personal routine. You must discover your favorite things to do that are also healthy and own that morning routine. It goes without saying that when you own the first part of your day, it gives you the confidence to step into the next one. You dare to face the boss or have the boldness to host the meeting that can bring investment into your company. Even more than that, your routine is something you do every day and is a space of comfort for your mind.

Make a list - Usually, a list will help keep you focussed on the tasks you have to do for your day. Often the best idea is to keep about five tasks on the list that must get done. You want to put high impact tasks on that list so that you are being productive and moving the needle on the goals you hope to achieve. There is something that happens when you commit to writing a daily list. It connects your thought process with these items, and it stays on your mind throughout the day, serving as a reminder that you must take care of these items. The brain becomes your reminder to help with your tasks. It makes you keep thinking about those tasks and may even draw up visual plans to help you start getting to work. If you've ever had a project due in the next 24 hours, you may be all too familiar with the prioritizing idea. Knowing you have 24 hours makes you think differently about the project. You ignore unnecessary thoughts and focus on only what is relevant for your project. You start to see that this project only needs specific inputs and people. And your brain helps you by connecting the dots to what you need. If you make a list, you activate a similar process, where you prioritize these five tasks for your day, and your brain will only focus on that for the day removing most distractions. You can choose to use an application on your phone to create your list or simply use a notepad, which you write a list on every day. If you want to kick it up a notch, you may find value in also writing your goal or wildly important target at the top of the page as a motivating factor.

Mindset management - If you would like to have consistent behavior learn how to manage your mind. The mind is a powerful tool but can also be a dangerous weapon where you can use it either for good in your life or destruction. When you opt to use your mindset for good, then you experience a better framework and system to use to lead your life. If you choose the alternative, then opportunities pass you by. For starters, when you manage your mind, it will help you to think more consistently and with values that create the foundation for your consistent behavior. This becomes especially true if you overthink a project's possibilities but never get down to work. It's time to start building better foundations in your mind by reframing your goal, and what's needed. When you reframe your objective and the value it will bring, you're helping your mind find out what you truly want. As it gets to know this, it becomes easier to help you meet that goal.

Curb self-doubt - You will find that when things are going well, there is the odd chance that self-doubt will start to creep in. You wonder if everything is going too well, so you begin to second guess yourself. You see problems everywhere with how you do things. It helps to know that you are not alone; we all feel these feelings of worry and self-doubt when we make progress. If you choose to let fear and self-doubt derail your progress, it becomes more challenging to get back on board, and you have to start back in the beginning again. When you experience self-doubt, it helps if you observe that feeling knowing it is just a feeling that hasn't impacted on your action. If you keep on doing, then self-doubt tends to dissolve. Another way to handle self-doubt is to face it head-on, and observe it in every stage without getting involved. Victor Frankl, a survivor of the Holocaust explains in his book "Man's search for meaning" that he survived the atrocities at the concentration camps because he could watch himself as though he were a separate entity. In this way, whatever happened to him, it could be compartmentalized and studied later. Your mind can also apply a similar tool, where you compartmentalize your self-doubt, study it at a later stage while you continue working without letting it disrupt you.

Ignore the feelings (for now) - Just do the task, and don't worry about how it makes you feel. The chances are that your feelings will always come back around, but the work still needs to get done. If you set the work aside and choose to do it at a later stage, what if you feel even worse? These are questions you can use in your self-talk. Your emotions are important, yes, but they can derail your ability to gain momentum. The thing about feelings is that they are fleeting, and most times, by managing your emotions by using work as a distraction, you will find that your well-being and mindset will shift. If you ever find yourself in analysis paralysis and unhelpful attitudes, it's time to employ a strategy to keep working even amidst the feeling. Focus on the task at hand, one action at a time. Stephen King, who wrote the book IT, is famous for his writing method, where he chooses that every day for a set number of hours, he will write even amidst the feelings that will inevitably creep up. Some days are amazing, and he writes pages and pages of his books while others are less than great, but at least he accomplished something. Once more, as a person who is prone to feel at any given time, you cannot be a slave to your feelings and choose to be productive instead.

These ideas will help you stay consistent daily as you plan for setbacks and manage your life appropriately to take them on. The rule is often that the more consistent you become, the better your chance to reach optimal levels of progress, and this will compound for you.

Reading from the greats

Have you ever worked with a person who was always

82

reading, and somehow they seemed to share the advice too. Their work output was excellent, and they were even up for the next promotion. If so, then a quick look into how reading from the greats may help you understand why this person was able to make progress. Firstly when you read books from influential people, you get to have a mentor by your side who has walked the path of success you hope to walk.

Think about Steve Jobs, who failed at a massive scale and was even kicked out of his own company. He had to fail to learn, and then he went ahead and created a new system they would use on Apple, namely NeXt, which was used on all Macs in the future. Even more than that, he went onto Pixar. He learned about their storytelling methodology, which he brought back to Apple and started creating launches of their products, which were based on storytelling. You see how reading about his story can bring you these insights about failure and how it can be a stepping stone to take back to your business.

Additionally, we can learn about their stories, but we can also learn from their habits. As we mentioned, earlier Bill Gates read 50 books a year while Warren Buffer spends 80% of his day reading. Not only do we learn from their habits but their personal stories. You get to read books by Elon Musk, who vividly describes his journey from Paypal to Tesla and how he handled business and success. The reading habit is where you get to see the steps successful people took to get their business started, how they made deals, and how they create discipline in their lives. Instead of paying for coaching and mentoring, you have that in a book that you can quickly page through for the lessons you need. Additionally, if a business person wrote a book, they also would have their content on their blog and YouTube so you can be sure to keep in touch with lessons in a variety of ways.

In a recent book highlighting the greatest entrepreneurs of this century, I learned more about the workings of entrepreneurs who did not work in the technological age. His name is John D Rockefeller, and he is one of the wealthiest people ever to walk this earth. How did he manage this and to build such an empire? He was, first and foremost, someone who was always interested in progress. Initially, he was a clerk who earned minimal wages but soon set his eyes on the oil industry.

He noticed that people needed oil for Kerosene and other by-products and swiftly found a way to capitalize by creating the Standard Oil Company in 1870. He stayed with the company for 27 years, eventually seeing it turn into a multimillion-dollar business. His motto was that he kept on learning, and understanding business, he created mastermind groups and read vociferously. This association with influential people was why he could quickly change strategy every time the government made new rules based on competition in the oil industry.

Aspire for the next stage of your life

When I think about a progressive approach to self-improvement, I have also to consider a future-focused mindset. This is where I look at where I'm going and how I'm going to get there. Some may call this your vision or goals, but for me, it's more than that. It's about what that vision can mean for your life and how it can take your standard of living to new heights. Perhaps you're living from paycheck to paycheck; then, your aspirations might be to be financially free and manage your money instead of your money managing you. You want to have total control of your income. It can be done, but you have to envision a better stage of your life. How would you go about doing that?

First, you should know where you currently stand and how your life has been going so far. It means taking an audit of your life, including personal goals, finances, and hopes for the future. Once you have these aspects in hand, you're in a great position to dig into your dreams for the future. Think about blue-sky ideas where you can do anything and be anything provided; it is part of your key strengths. If you consider your strengths, you can narrow your focus on the activities and goals that are possible and what you love to do. This refinement of your goal will help you create a bold vision for the next stage of life. It will help to truly get to the heart of what you would love to see for you and your family in 5, 10, and 15 years.

The next stage of your life could mean that you must make a career change, or it could mean that you choose to start a business or opt to get a promotion at work. There are so many iterations of the dream that you need to scope out. Your vision is the one that makes you the happiest. I've often found with goals, that when they are not close to your heart or what you are passionate about, you don't see the energy or the enthusiasm to follow through daily. However, if your goals are bold and scare you and excite you at the same time, you might just be onto something. I urge you then to take a moment to imagine the best version of your life. Are you living where you currently live and who are your friends?

Do you see the best version of your life with more freedom and what kind of freedom? By thinking through these questions, it will bring to mind what your desire is for life. Now that you understand your desire, you may need to fine-tune it to suit your capabilities to seek help to make it a reality. If, for example, you are currently an employee, then look at how your current situation can get you to the next destination. If it cannot help you, then let's consider a few options that may help. Your options could be that it's time to look at alternative opportunities such as starting a side hustle for yourself, perhaps making a side income that can help you quickly invest that money. It could mean that you need to upgrade your education by increasing your writing, programming, or marketing skills. Again your strengths will play a role here, and when you lean into those strengths, it's easy to see what you are good at. If at this point, you want to get clarity on your strengths, a great tool is using Strengths Finder by Gallup, which will give the five key strengths that will help you succeed. Examples of strengths include aspects like strategic thinking or futuristic. If you have a skillset of strategic thinking, it means you could have excellent leadership ability, and that might prompt you to take up a leadership role in your company. Alternatively, if you are futuristic, where you often think about what the future may hold, consider looking into careers where technology might be right up your alley like AI programming.

Remember, it's about thinking up ideas that will work for you in the best way. When you finally see the concept that is possible, and that will work for you, it becomes a choice of either making it your next stage or living with regret because you did not try. All in all, the process of introspection will yield many ideas about your future states. It's then about you refining those ideas and making it tangible.

A few years ago, I was consulting for a business where the company was not growing. Looking at the data, I found excellent performance in the company during some months while other months lacked. In my findings, I noted that the level of inconsistency was derailing the progress. Based on this data, I was able to go into the company and work with the individuals, and I noticed something startling again. The first was that people in the company did not have discipline, rigor, and structure. In short, they were inconsistent, and their daily efforts were not similar. On some days their productivity would be 50% while on other days it would be 150%. I knew there was a need to update the standard in that the expectation is that employees should have 95% productivity daily.

To help the teams, I showed them that their work hours were inconsistent daily, and if they improved those by applying better habits such as starting and finishing work at the same time, it would make a world of difference. After a month or so, the team began to see the difference in their habits and found that they were making better progress every day, and they could see an upward trend in their outputs. Why did I share this example with you? I wanted to contextualize the process of progress and how it shows up when you start to take consistency in your work and life seriously.

Key Takeaways

Keeping consistent should be your motto, and generating that consistency should be a daily focus, where you review what's keeping you from consistency. If you can understand the derailing actions, you can make plans to remove those actions from your day. Aspects such as planning and ensuring you have everything scheduled with daily to-do lists keep you in check. Furthermore, your consistency is based on your attachment to your goals and how connected you are to them. You must spend some time in your morning routine dedicated to visualizing your goals, writing them down, and considering some actions to make them come to life. This will be a habit you build, and the more you keep your discipline and consistency, the better results you will see.

Reading from the greats will help you immensely. This is all about how your reading should zone into business figures or inspirational leaders who have walked the path before you. It should be that you read autobiographies from the likes of Elon Musk, Bill Gates, and Richard Branson, who have managed to achieve business and life success and maintained this over several years.

Aspire for the next stage of your life in everything you do. The goal here is always to think one step ahead of your current stage in life. If you haven't yet reached your current goal, know that you've included all the inputs, then it's only time that will show you the results, you have to keep moving forward on your path. Make your future plans boldly and let it drive you as you wake up every morning, ready to take on another day. Motivate yourself through your reading, your mastermind group, and your instinct needed to reach new levels as an entrepreneur.

Action steps

1. Audit your day by tracking all of the tasks you do, and how much time you spend on them. You can spend a week auditing and write down as much as possible. Once done, collate the results, and group your time and efforts. You may want to look at categories like productive work, social media, downtime, and sleep.
2. Once you've audited your day, find areas where you need to reduce time spent, such as social media time, and allocate that time to productive work. Schedule that time in your calendar, so you know it has to be done.
3. Commit to making a daily to-do list where you list five critical tasks that if they get done, they will move your life and business forward.
4. Think long term and visualize where you see yourself in the next year, and how you feel. Set plans into motion by looking at where your strengths meet your passion. Work towards doing this for the next stage of your life.

The reality is that going on a journey of progression has always been a lucrative and exciting path. If you choose it, you have to be willing to keep moving even when things don't go your way. If you decide to stay on a path of daily consistency, many great things will start to manifest for your life, and this will also help grow you as a person. The only thing left to say is that life is one big rollercoaster that takes you to fantastic highs and brings you to daring lows. Most of the ride, some people choose to close their eyes because they are afraid to look. They miss out on the great adventure, and they never get to learn how to progress and build themselves amidst the ups and downs of life.

Similarly, that's how you can look at your current state and everything in it. You can opt to see it as an adventure where you are getting to do everything you love and learning the much-needed skill along the way. Let's proceed to the final chapter, and I'll show you how to remove your limitations and push boundaries for your life.

CHAPTER 7
Push Boundaries in Your Life

Congratulations, you have now reached the final part of this book. You will get to look into the procedure for starting life in a new way using this self-improvement guide. This will help you see that applying new principles to your life can help you update your mindset. Perhaps when you first opened this book, you thought that it would be a daunting task to improve yourself, but over time and reading through the text, you've seen that it can be done quicker than you thought possible.

In this section, the goal is to start pushing the boundaries for your life. If you are currently comfortable with the experience, it may be that you are also missing out on an opportunity to change your success rate.

Contents

Keep focused
Discipline is your friend
Planning is half the work

Keep focussed

I know that there are many critical principles sprinkled

throughout this guide, and it can be easy to get sidetracked onto a new topic in every chapter. That's why I want to urge you to keep your focus as you progress. How can you do this when a million different things are demanding your attention. You need only look around you at the smartphone, your Television, or your laptop, which offers you streaming on demand, hundreds of channels, and social media. These are options that are available for a relatively low price and can have you spending hours engaging. The reality is that many social media applications have teams of people trying to make the app more addictive so you can spend longer on it, and this always equates to some sort of revenue for those companies. So how can you outsmart the focus stealers in favor of keeping your focus?

There are a few tools that never fail to help, which I've included for you below:

Concentration timer - As the name suggests, this will help you time your work and chimes every few minutes to remind you to stay focussed. This can be helpful, especially if you have a wandering mind, as it brings you right back to focus. The good news is that it works well for meditation too.

Rescue time - This tool helps to bring you back to motivation by making you think about your actions. It offers us a report where it tracks how much time you are using on a variety of sites and makes you reflect on your focus. It works by monitoring the windows you have open and have accessed so far. Usually, it will serve up a graph showing your day.

Digg deeper - With billions of websites floating around the internet, it might be hard to keep track of everything. This tool helps gather your favorite information, including social media updates, emails, and content that you wish to see. It saves you time and prevents the manic email checking mechanism.

These tools are great ways to keep you focussed on the usual demands we see in our day, but it still needs your discipline to do this. How can you take it one step further?

You can choose to get rid of distractions, and that usually means you take some form of an effort to start by moving items that are known distractors of your time. Examples include moving over to a quieter area, where there are no distractions or turning off your mobile phone. Many people at the office have closed their office doors and shared emails around distractions with their colleagues to create awareness.

If you have eliminated all distractions and still find it challenging to keep focus, you could treat yourself to a strong cup of coffee to get the focus juices flowing again. Studies have shown that when you drink caffeinated beverages in small doses, it has a good impact on your ability to keep your mind on the task. A word of warning here is that you should always think about drinking coffee in moderation to ensure you keep from feeling anxious or nervous. In other words, too much coffee may have the opposite of the desired effect.

A great tool that has been in existence from the late '80s is the Pomodoro. The technique works on the premise that you can use time effectively if you space out your focus time accordingly. You have to time yourself focusing as well as taking breaks. In this way, you use timing to train your brain to stay on task for short periods. You can easily use the timer on your phone or a kitchen timer if it's available. Now you are ready to start trying out the Pomodoro method by setting your timer for 25 minutes. You can start working, and when the buzzer goes, you can take 5-minute breaks — once done, set the time again, and start working for 25 minutes. Once you've had four rounds of 25-minute sessions, take an extended break of 20 minutes. This is an excellent method for studying, but also people in the business setting have found it works great for projects that have a tight deadline.

While I've mentioned a few other aspects, such as getting the right amount of sleep and eating a well-balanced diet, the other tool that gets missed is the batching method which we discussed in chapter 1 and I'll bring you more detail here. Batching is not a new concept where you group work that is similar and set aside time to do this work. For example, if you have work involving spreadsheets and data collection, you may need to set aside those types of tasks for a few hours and only work with these. This will ensure that you adequately apply your brain capacity and not drain your energy unnecessarily on scattered tasks. If you create content for your business, it means you have many types of content to produce. Instead of setting aside days where you provide written, video, and audio content. You could group all of your written content for the month and produce those within two days. Once those are done for the next few days, you can focus on video content and so forth. Then you don't scatter your focus. You use it to zone in on an area and maximize the output. When you start batching your work, you save time, but you also manage your focus and energy much better.

The reality is that you have many priorities in a day, and when you add a lack of sleep or a somewhat challenging time in your week, it could be a recipe for disaster. You can still choose to manage your focus more effectively. The tips highlighted in this section, and the tools provided will be sure to help you get rid of those distractions and win back your focus. You will soon learn about the activities that bring you the most attention, which will help you choose better methods and tools.

If you can master the art of focus, the benefits are immense, where you get to reduce the stress that is present in your body, and that stems from procrastination. This is related to the fear of doing the work and presents as a lack of focus. Another benefit that is often overlooked is that you start to improve your communication skills and self-confidence. You even get better at the decision-making process, while your creative ability expands.

Discipline is your friend

One of the better skills to develop in life is your ability to be disciplined and stay the course of a task you said you would. Most people are not born disciplined they learn discipline through bad experiences or where their parents cultivated it in them. If you don't have much self-discipline, everything becomes so much for challenging, and when you have it, it feels like you can do many things. It may start with you wanting to stop putting off work tasks like projects and doing that as and when they arrive. Then you felt the motivation of completing the job, and you started to see that self-discipline could be applied to many aspects of life, such as exercising and eating healthy. You may be surprised by the transformation that can occur when you've cultivated a sense of discipline in your life. While we can see it is an important skill to have, it can be challenging to get started. Therefore, I want to share some of the best tools you can use to create discipline for yourself.

Look at your motivation - There can be many reasons you wish to create discipline in yourself. Perhaps in the distant past, you were not a great student because you did not have a goal or a driving force. Later on, in life, you started to contemplate a better future for you and your loved ones. Keeping this in mind, you knew you needed to begin creating discipline and doing what you said you were going to do, no matter how bad a situation might get.

Little actions - While every one of us would love to do things on a big scale, finishing a massive project in a week or singing at an opera - it's impossible since practice takes time, and honing your craft also needs your time. I suggest that you start by doing small things that link to your discipline. Perhaps right now you're waking up at 7 am and rushing to get to work with barely any time to plan your day. Here's an idea. What if you decided to set your alarm for just 30 minutes earlier and read a few pages in a book instead. Those pages will quickly accumulate, and you will read a 300 pages book in no time. Yet, the little actions are about the small changes you are making that go by without noticing. Eventually, those small changes become significant results.

Focus on others - At times, you may struggle to find the motivation to keep on going in terms of your work or personal life. The motivation is simply not there. What if you choose to do it for others where you say that doing your work will benefit some else's life. The people in your life whom you care about the most. The reframing of this is making those closest to you the reason you choose to work out or do the work. If you're a musician, then the music you make will bring joy to others and light up their day, and that could make you inspired to keep on having the discipline to make music. You indeed benefit in most of the ideas above, but you're also thinking of it in service of those closest to you, and that drive to get it completed becomes stronger.

Success is not linear - The more you try new ideas and experiment, then there will be more failure. It does not make you a failure, far from it. You are someone who knows that failure is part of success. The more you fail, the more you learn. When you see success plotted on a graph, people may think it's a straight line graph that goes to the top with much hassle. That's not the case, as success is a combination of many highs and lows, and it's about you know you will fail, so you have to embrace this and know that everything will soon turn around. You should not become disheartened by the failure and let it take away your focus and discipline you've cultivated so far.

Call a friend - This can equally apply to a family member too. If you seek out discipline, it may be that you are not at the level you hoped to reach. You see that people are progressing so far on their journey to discipline while you are still in the early stages. Firstly, don't compare yourself. You could be looking at someone after their 200th attempt, and when you make a comparison, you're using the wrong scale to do so. Decide then and there that people can help you, and you need only call your mentors' friends to give you perspective on your approach to work. They may show you that you have the opportunity to be a better and more disciplined teacher.

More and more, the opportunity is presenting itself where you can be a more disciplined person. You can read books about the topic, and have a mentor guide you. These are paid tools and methods, but often the best tool is to honestly introspect and find out the reasons why you do not have the discipline to follow through. Frequently, it has been with you since a child where you were so scared of failure that you left things to the last minute. You hoped one day it would get better, but it never did. So much so that when you reached adulthood, you tried everything always to get the job done, to do the work, but it left you frustrated and exhausted physically and mentally. The main reason this happened is that you have not befriended your discipline. You see it when you look at the pile of work you have to do, and then mentally start seeing it as a mountain instead of a growing area of work that needs to get done. The more you see it as a mountain instead of a step by step process, it creates a feeling of resistance in you, and you often do not have a bias for action. This lack of effort then causes you to feel exhausted even though you have not done anything to move your goals forward. The science behind it is even more startling. We often look at discipline as a form of will-power, where we have to ensure something gets done by forcing ourselves to do it. If you have to force yourself to do something you're just going to expend more energy that you could be using to do that task instead. The reality is that tasks are always going to be painfully dull when you think about it, sometimes it will be that way for the next 15 to 20 minutes, but if you absorb yourself in the task and make it a priority, then the job starts to become a little more interesting.

Here's a process you can use to get more discipline in your life:

1. **Get started** - A little progress is better than no progress. if you simply commit to opening the first document or typing that first email or making that first call, you'll see it's not as painful as you imagined. Suddenly, starting could lead to you making a second call and writing another email. If you never start, you never get the opportunity to see the process in action or see that those starting moments are the way to finish any task. Will it be painful to start? Yes, it will be emotionally draining, but there are some ways that you can look past the pain and choose to keep doing instead. Also, I want to add that by starting; it doesn't mean you will complete the task. Not by a long shot, you may take several days, but if you keep that in mind, the progress you make will remind you that you are moving closer to your goals.

2. **You will never have more time** - I wanted to give you some perspective on this one, where every day that passes, your life on this planet gets shorter and shorter. For example, when you were in college, you could spend endless amounts of time so that you could spend it studying or doing nothing.

Think about all the time you wasted, but as you get older and your job starts to take up more of your time, or your family life is busier, your free time decreases, and you do not have the luxury of wasting time. Every moment counts, and when you don't do something productive, you will look back and realize you could have and should have done more. The idea here is that you should start now. Imagine how many things you could have accomplished if you applied this framework ten years ago, and it will give you the realization that you have to get going.

3. **Take a walk daily** - This seems easy, but if you have to do it every day, you have to keep a promise to yourself. It's deliberately easy as you start to see that even the simple task of walking becomes a chore. Everything we do in our minds is considered boring, challenging when done a hundred times. In this case, you simply have to know that this is going to be boring but have to do it. If your mind starts to think: "What if I just skip it for today," then pick up your stuff and shoes and simply ignore it and go for your walk. You'll find that every time you go walking when you don't want to, you build up some form of discipline that tells your body to take an extra step even if every part of you is saying, "This is boring."

4. **Embrace the group** - If you work with more people, you start to hold each other accountable for the work. This accountability serves to help everyone to feel motivated and keep doing knowing that the group will succeed. How could this play out? Study with friends, have project meetings at coffee shops and set roles and responsibilities for each team member, and review the task list week to see if actions are being completed. If not, then have a rewards system or punishment system. An example of punishment is allocating

the person who does not do the task to buy everyone drinks. It's also more enjoyable when you know that you are all in this together.

5. **Set a target** - Your target of work per day could be that you finish two pages of a report a day, and push to do those two pages no matter what happens. People don't start because they are too scared that the finished product is not going to look great and that fear waits for conditions to get perfect. It will never be perfect, but through starting, you can create and fix and update as much as possible. Your targets should also be more visible in that you can write a goal and the date on a whiteboard or keep it in your journal, where when you are done, you can scratch it off, which can be satisfying.

6. **Decide and stick to it** - There are certain values that we all live by, and these values govern if we do something. You have to choose your values then and keep reinforcing it. What if one of your values was to decide that you would always do a task, no matter how difficult or boring it seems. You must do it. In the beginning, you know that it will be hard to do it. You will watch yourself procrastinate continuously, but you will start to do it slowly, but surely it will improve the way you approach that task and every other task. If it's boring or challenging, then that is your trigger to do.

7. **Be productive** - That sounds easy at first, but being productive is harder than you think. Inside is the need for comfort and to always relax or take it easy. Yet even though we love to take it easy, when you start to get productive, it's hard to stop. The feeling of achieving and doing is addictive. Then when you're busy, it makes it ten times easier to do a task you dread.

Planning is half the work

If you're not good at planning, it might be time to focus your attention on this section. Planning is a fine art that can end up helping you in the long run. The act of planning is somewhat like creating a blueprint for what's to come in your life. It's the instruction manual for the next stages, and all you have to do is follow. Think about those spy movies where the hero often is briefed on the nature of the mission, and shown some of the villains that will present themselves, as well as the difficulties of the mission. This person must then consider all aspects and look at what they need to do to overcome it. What does the person do? They ask questions, and clarify and give input to the person briefing them. Once done and all the items are answered, and they are confident in the plan, they build a feeling of resolution knowing that they have the plan, they have considered everything and can feel confident no matter what comes their way. In the absence of this stage, the hero of the movie would go into the battlefield without a plan. Everything would be a mess, they would be continuously surprised, and they'd have to think of an idea and also get into action mode. That's too difficult for the brain and makes their job all the more difficult.

Similarly, your life is a mission you have to plan for. It's a mission where you have to create a brief for the challenges that will come your way. You have to look at the villains in your life, like procrastination, comfort, unhealthy relationships, and more. Once you understand these aspects, you will feel more confident approaching these enemies and tackle them head-on.

How do you plan for success effectively:

Know your strengths - You would have done the Strengths Finder test by Gallup, and perhaps discovered your core strengths and had time to reflect upon them. Often in the assessment, they give you action steps to enhance those strengths. Use that to your advantage where you automatically know what you will be good at and what will be your nemesis when it comes to tasks. To make it more practical, if you are a more big picture thinker, then working with detailed tasks like creating data reports could be your Achilles heel. Instead of doing all those tasks on your own, partner with someone who has their strengths within a specific field. If you work with this person, you can have complementary skills that could benefit the project. Alternatively, you could choose to hire an expert for that work while focusing on the big picture ideas. You can only know this when you lean into your strengths to use this information to your advantage. When you lean into your strengths, you make your ability to do the task much more comfortable and allow for less frustration. You could then always keep a list of strengths around so that you can reference back when you feel a sense of frustration with the task, and then this will give you the understanding to keep going or delegate that task.

Accept the challenges - Too often, we expect that tasks will be easier than they are. When we have this unhealthy expectation, it's more likely that we'll be disappointed when the job is difficult and takes longer than expected. It's so easy to give up and leave the task to the last minute. What if you chose to look at every job as unique and challenging, instead of deciding it will be easy. You know that you will make mistakes, and it will make you frustrated, but at least you are mentally prepared for these mistakes and can quickly work at it instead of giving up. I often see this when working with people that planning becomes the most tedious task for them. It is somewhat jarring as they have never done it before. If we take a step back and understand why we should plan and how it's essential, it shifts the framework, and the process goes smoothly. One pervasive aspect is people getting frustrated because they think they are machines and want to fit too many tasks into one day. It's important to be kind to yourself, knowing that you will need rest, sleep, and time for yourself, or you will feel burnout. The consistency and discipline sections will immensely help you go back and review those as you will never need to burn the midnight oil if you are consistent.

Find the enemies to success - Look at the barriers to your success. This could be that you have left your smartphone notifications on, and every time it goes off you check it, and it steals your focus. Turn those notifications off, and only check your phone once you have finished a batch of work. Perhaps you and your significant other are misaligned in terms of your goals. This manifests in bickering because you are always working and can be emotionally exhausting. It might be time to talk to your partner and find common ground to avoid the arguments and help you stay focused and on track. This is all-important in the planning stage. If you leave it too late, you could end up blowing up in frustration or anger and impacting your relationship. Look towards your environment; if you study or the working room is always a mess, it's time to get organized. The situation can tell a lot about your mental state and can even breed unhealthy working habits. Make it a priority to declutter every area you work in so that your mind is not focussed on the clutter but the task at hand.

Make a system - You may be tempted to borrow someone else's system. I mean, if it worked for them, then it could work for you too. Avoid that and instead create a system that works for your unique needs. Are you someone who works best with imagery and visual cues, then make a vision board easier to connect with. Alternatively, use color codes systems such as sticky notes for to-do lists on a whiteboard. When writing lists also use a variety of colors for your purposes. Or you may need detail then use spreadsheet programs like excel to help you organize your lists and include deadlines and everything you need to do. There is no right way on how you should make a plan. There is just a way that works best for you.

Planning is fundamental, and one of the ways that can help to focus your mind. Einstein told us that if he had an hour to solve a problem, he would spend 55 minutes thinking about it. How can you apply this to your life? The planning phase is the problem phase, and the more time you spend here, the easier it will be to execute and get your stuff done. Mostly planning is half the work done. You know you have planned well when you look back at all you had to do and how easy it seemed, and you feel a sense of pride and confidence in your genius planning skills. Therefore, I urge you to take that time and start to plan what you wish to do. It will be entirely dependent on your needs and is the starting point of how you can begin to become a more systematic person who consistently gets the job done.

Key Takeaways

Keeping focused so you can keep your balance is a fundamental part of pushing your boundaries to self-improvement. You will find your focus was a redeeming factor when everyone else around you was swayed by a new shiny object. The focus can come in handy when you set your mind on a goal you wish to achieve and follow right through till the end. You will find many focus stealers along the way, but none can remove your ability to keep your eyes on the prize if you follow the focus formula highlighted within this chapter.

Discipline is your friend in the best of ways. It's guaranteed that if you keep discipline by your side and keep it as your guide, you will be able to accomplish many things all the faster. Discipline means that the little things matter, like your consistent approach, the time you wake up, and staying true to what you said you would do. When you cultivate discipline, you create a habit of excellence, and that tends to become a guiding light on your way to self-improvement.

Planning is half the work, and the other half is everything else mentioned in this book. Planning and this includes the research of your journey to self-improvement should be the way you first start. Use tools like mentors, planning guides, and idea banks to create a solid master plan that you execute. You always have to build strategies to make it happen. Think of this as your blueprint for success.

Actions steps

1. Review the previous sections of this book. Look at actions in each chapter and observe your mindset since you've reached the end of this book.

2. Bring everything you've learned together, such as creating a masterplan for success and filling in the tactical steps. Make your goals smart and review them weekly/monthly/yearly.

3. Get an accountability buddy who you can share the highs and lows of your journey with, and start to create a mastermind group that you can use for support.

CONCLUSION
Now, It's Your Turn

Many people have asked me over the years about their self-improvement process. I often think it is a question of habits, and those who have the best practices will make much more pronounced improvements than others. You see people or more inclined to keep getting better at every stage. You engage a person working for a corporate company and ask them about their last performance report, and they will tell you that they did not do as well as they would have liked. They may even start telling you how their boss is not exactly their best friend. In that way, they are making many excuses for not improving. Let's always aim to focus on gradual improvements because when we as human beings see improvement, we get hopeful, and when we get confident, we can do more and create more of the best work of our lives.

Think about people who are professionals in sports like a gymnast who wins gold at the Olympics? Were they gifted from a young age? Sure, they innately had that strength, but you know what set them head and shoulders above others? It's the fact that they made improvements every day; they practiced and ensured that they mastered what they had been taught. It was about their mindset, their diligence, and their overall attentiveness to detail that brought them close to their goals. As the gymnast grew, they inherently could see the progress they were making, and all those incremental improvements stacked up, and finally, they could see that they had won a gold medal.

But let me ask you this. What is the difference between the gold medalist and the silver medalist? They had an excellent performance, they are world-class athletes, but somehow the gold medalist won. It's a thought-provoking question in a world where 0.2 of a score makes a difference, and subjectivity could also factor in. You see, it was inherently that one had studied their craft more, practiced more, and on that particular day, everything they had done in life as a gymnast was summed up like a mathematical equation and provided the right answer. The winning answer. Overall, this book's main idea is to show you that self-improvement is a constant process that needs you to make progress. It requires consistency, and it needs habits and your commitment to doing better. You cannot merely hope for better days and be better, nor can you participate from the sidelines - you need to take an active stance and move forwards and upwards.

Also, congratulations on taking the first step towards a new venture in your life. You've decided to be the controller of your destiny. Now the universe is gathering all of its strength to help you along. In these pages, you have seen stories of courage and success. You have also seen failures that became successes, but most importantly, you have seen the tools that made it so. In this way, the aim is always to help you create a practical toolkit for yourself, even when you put down this book. You will always have a blueprint for self-improvement because the journey of self-improvement is never-ending. It's exciting, exhilarating, and frankly, it will change your whole life if you let it.

Let's recap and add some parting comments before you make your ways towards your life's goals. Always remember that taking control is a personal decision that must be considered and measured in all areas. You must seek out the challenges in your life, face them head-on, and decide to take control. We discussed that a family could not do it for you, nor can your friends. You must do it, and you must be bold enough to choose to take control. The good news is that when you take control, great things will start to happen for you. You will begin to see that the cloudy feelings you have seem to vanish and you're left staring out a clear front window and looking at your wondrous and magnificent future ahead.

Your level of control taking can inspire you and it becomes mandatory for you to set a destination for where you wish to go. If you don't choose one, life will do it for you. If you don't select a target, you will land up just about anywhere and live with it. So I urge you to follow the plan to choose a destination. This idea will give you the structures needed to select a goal that will make you proud in 5,10 or 15 years. You will also use this destination vision to propel you forward when times get rough. Your destination is the fire inside you that burns brightly, urging you to keep going.

By now, you would have seen an uptick in your productivity. Where you were too exhausted to do anything now, everything can be done quickly and accurately. Why may you ask? Well, having a plan immediately sets the tone for everything else. Yes, some days you may not always feel like following the procedure, that's quite fine. We're all human, after all, but for the most part, you will never forget your productivity tools and use it to enhance how you operate in your work, business, or personal life.

You should start to see your relationships improve immensely, where people would avoid you before and now you have great conversations with them. This is serving to boost your networks and bring all sorts of opportunities into your life. You're becoming someone who people love to engage with and help. Your projects are moved quickly through the process, and people are clamoring to work with you. This is what happens when you follow the advice on building interpersonal relationships, and now you will start to see the fruits of your labor.

Finally, you can reach a new summit. It's the height of continuous improvement and progressing either in business or in your job. If you're an employee, you become obsessed with improving, always re-iterating, and showing the best progress is being made. So much so that your enthusiasm is catching. People follow you, and you lead the way because you decided to make improvements in your life.

Could you imagine that taking charge of your life and getting better at every step would bring you to this point? Yet it has, and now you can start to push the boundaries of your life. You work on the assumption that everything is possible if you are willing to try. You also know that you can always learn along the way, and you do not need to be the master of everything. You can leverage the people you know who can help you.

This is only the beginning for your new life centered around self-improvement. This is no small feat knowing that so many who have gone before you have failed. You pushed forwards and decided to keep on trying, keep on going, and getting better. I commend you for this dedication and urge you to continue to be an entrepreneur in your life.

REFERENCES

Skillsyouneed.com. 2020. *Interpersonal Skills.* [online] Skillsyouneed. Available at: <https://www.skillsyouneed.com/interpersonal-skills.html> [Accessed 19 June 2020].

Bridges, F., 2017. *10 Ways To Build Confidence.* [online] Forbes. Available at: <https://www.forbes.com/sites/francesbridges/2017/07/21/10-ways-to-build-confidence/#229c47133c59> [Accessed 19 June 2020].

Collinsdictionary.com. n.d. *Mutual Benefit Definition And Meaning | Collins English Dictionary.* [online] Available at: <https://www.collinsdictionary.com/dictionary/english/mutual-benefit> [Accessed 19 June 2020].

Debt.org. 2019. [online] Available at: <https://www.debt.org/advice/emotional-effects/> [Accessed 19 June 2020].

Discoveryinaction.com.au. 2014. [online] Available at: <http://www.discoveryinaction.com.au/wp-content/uploads/2014/05/emotional-intelligence.png> [Accessed 19 June 2020].

Dodd, C., 2018. *10 Tools To Stay Focused That Are Actually Helpful.* [online] Turbinehq.com. Available at: <https://www.turbinehq.com/blog/tools-to-stay-focused>

[Accessed 3 July 2020].

Eaton-Cardone, M., Ganado, M. and Hernandez, J., 2019. *3 Inspiring Lessons We Can Learn From Jim Carrey About The Law Of Attraction.* [online] Addicted 2 Success. Available at: <https://addicted2success.com/life/3-inspiring-lessons-we-can-learn-from-jim-carrey-about-the-law-of-attraction/> [Accessed 19 June 2020].

Focusing with Fiona Parr. 2019. *Benefits Of Focusing - Fiona Parr.* [online] Available at: <https://fionaparr-focusing.co.uk/benefits/> [Accessed 3 July 2020].

Gates, B., 2019. *5 Summer Books And Other Things To Do At Home.* [online] gatesnotes.com. Available at: <https://www.gatesnotes.com/About-Bill-Gates/Summer-Books-2020> [Accessed 3 July 2020].

Harvard Business Review. n.d. *A Way To Plan If You're Bad At Planning.* [online] Available at: <https://hbr.org/2017/07/a-way-to-plan-if-youre-bad-at-planning> [Accessed 3 July 2020].

Healthline. n.d. *How To Stay Focused: 10 Tips To Improve Your Focus And Concentration.* [online] Available at: <https://www.healthline.com/health/mental-health/how-to-stay-focused#take-breaks> [Accessed 3 July 2020].

Inc.com. 2017. *How To Reach The Next Stage Of Your Personal Evolution.* [online] Available at: <https://www.inc.com/benjamin-p-hardy/how-to-reach-the-next-stage-of-your-personal-evolu.html> [Accessed 3 July 2020].

Jack Canfield. n.d. *Visualization Techniques To Manifest Desired Outcomes | Jack Canfield.* [online] Available at: <https://www.jackcanfield.com/blog/visualize-and-affirm-your-desired-outcomes-a-step-by-step-guide/> [Accessed 19 June 2020].

James Clear. n.d. *How To Break A Bad Habit (And Replace It With A*

Good One). [online] Available at: <https://jamesclear.com/how-to-break-a-bad-habit> [Accessed 3 July 2020].

James Clear. n.d. *The 3 R's Of Habit Change: How To Start New Habits That Actually Stick*. [online] Available at: <https://jamesclear.com/three-steps-habit-change> [Accessed 3 July 2020].

Lifehack. 2020. *How To Organize Your Life: 10 Habits Of Really Organized People*. [online] Available at: <https://www.lifehack.org/articles/productivity/how-organize-your-life-10-habits-really-organized-people.html> [Accessed 19 June 2020].

McCreary, M., 2020. *The 3 Most Consistent Businesses From The Franchise 500 List*. [online] Entrepreneur. Available at: <https://www.entrepreneur.com/article/314072> [Accessed 3 July 2020].

Medium. 2016. *What Can We Learn From Henry Ford About Productivity?*. [online] Available at: <https://medium.com/my-productivity-kit/what-can-we-learn-from-henry-ford-about-productivity-3efe475bda6e> [Accessed 19 June 2020].

Medium. 2018. *How To Be Outrageously Consistent | 7 Tips To Be Consistently Consistent*. [online] Available at: <https://medium.com/the-mission/how-to-be-outrageously-consistent-7-tips-to-be-consistently-consistent-a32fd1c0a250> [Accessed 3 July 2020].

Mindtools.com. 2020. *How Can I Stop Procrastinating?: Overcoming The Habit Of Delaying Important Tasks*. [online] Available at: <https://www.mindtools.com/pages/article/newHTE_96.htm> [Accessed 19 June 2020].

Paine, N., n.d. *Why Michael Jordan Was The Best*. [online] FiveThirtyEight. Available at:

<https://fivethirtyeight.com/features/why-michael-jordan-was-the-best/> [Accessed 3 July 2020].

Planio. 2019. *The 21 Daily Routines And Habits Of Highly Productive Founders And Creatives | Planio.* [online] Available at: <https://plan.io/blog/daily-routines/> [Accessed 19 June 2020].

The Law Of Attraction. n.d. *What Is The Law Of Attraction? And How To Use It Effectively.* [online] Available at: <https://www.thelawofattraction.com/what-is-the-law-of-attraction/> [Accessed 19 June 2020].

Thompson, S., 2016. *7 Ways To Persist When Everything In You Wants To Give Up.* [online] SUCCESS. Available at: <https://www.success.com/7-ways-to-persist-when-everything-in-you-wants-to-give-up/> [Accessed 19 June 2020].

Vocabulary.com. 2020. *Control - Dictionary Definition.* [online] Available at: <https://www.vocabulary.com/dictionary/control> [Accessed 19 June 2020].

Zenhabits.net. n.d. *A Guide To Developing The Self-Discipline Habit : Zen Habits.* [online] Available at: <https://zenhabits.net/self-discipline/> [Accessed 3 July 2020].